FUGITIVE HEART

~

TheOgrePoet

PublishAmerica
Baltimore

ISBN: 1-60474-160-0
PUBLISHED BY PUBLISHAMERICA, LLLP
www.publishamerica.com
Baltimore

Printed in the United States of America

FUGITIVE HEART

~

TheOgrePoet

IN LOVING MEMORY

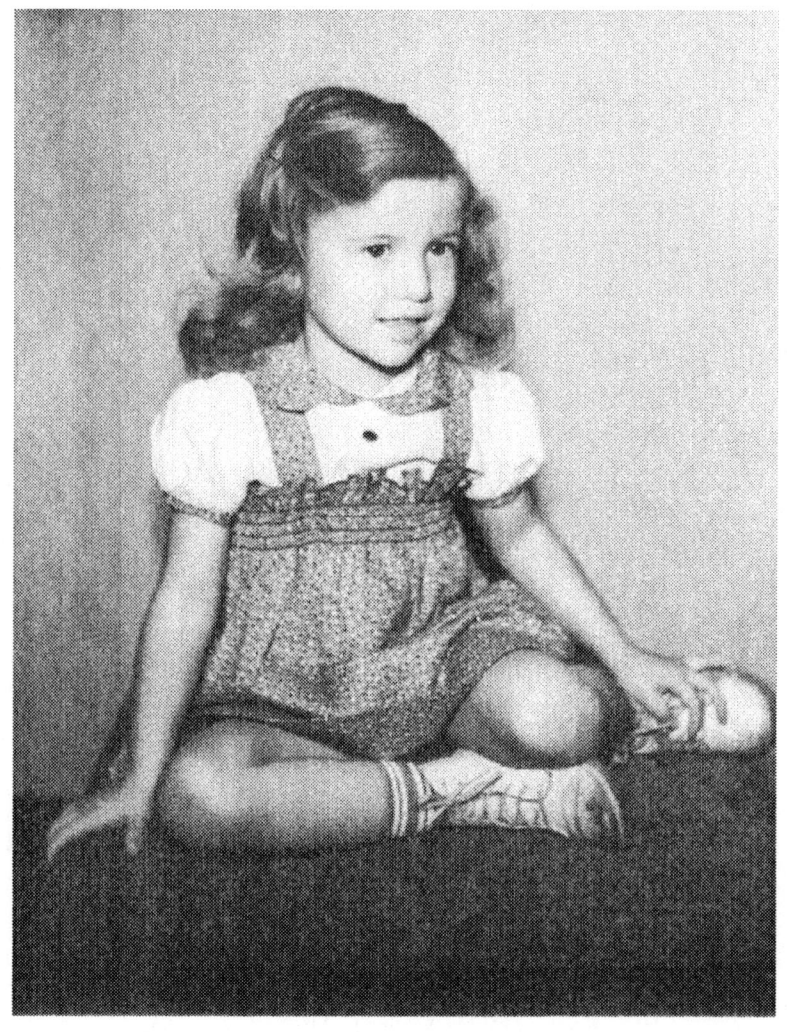

SHIRLEY ANN IMMEL
1935 – 2004

WE MISS YOU MOM

Acknowledgments

I would like to give special thanks to many people for their long-time support, love and understanding that allowed me to fulfill the dream come true of having these works published.

To my wife Paula for her understanding, support, love and friendship through all the crazy nights of writing I thank you. I know sometimes it was not easy to understand this dream but your tolerance and patience are truly appreciated.

My sons Richard and Jeremy, I know its not cool to have your dad be a poet, but your playful rhymes and silliness through all this truly inspired me, thank you.

To my princess, my daughter Melanie, your smile each day causes me to press on and see the sunshine on the darkest of days.

To dad; I can never thank you enough for all you have done for me over the years, I love you.

Special Thanks:

To Tracey Dee, I do not know what I would have done all these years without you reading and asking, "what in the hell does that mean?" You are a special human being and a shining light for all around you. Thank you for being you.

To Da Queen of Kewl, Tonya, it is hard to believe we have been friends for five years. Your support and friendship have been such an inspiration through all this time, I can never thank you enough.

To Heather my long-time friend, you have so much inspiration to share with so many through your art and your words. The world is a better place to have you within it my friend.

I would also like to thank those that donated their talents with photos and artwork, their names and websites are listed on the photo credits page. Please go support these folks, as they are incredible artists one and all.

Also to Deborah Lee Foley, J.A. McCrea, and Dannielle Diorrio for so graciously donating your time to help me edit this amassing of words, thoughts and ideas.

BASICS

The savory taste of your lips so divine...
Feasting delicately upon your delectable skin
One nibble from the neck may always suffice
Or should a sample from the curve of the hips
Develop goose bumps and chills to entice
> *...is all the communion this man needs*

Tears of joy forever travel cheeks tracts...
Wading through life sun baked and alone
Aqueducts of feelings constantly ran dry
Then you arrived to fill my dust-covered cup
Easily quenching all long desired thirsts
Replenishing even the empty ducts within my eyes
> *...our lake of passion shall never recede*

Resiliency thrives within walls of devotion...
Safety from the maddening world around
Home is a place full of romance and cheer
Evil winds shall never seep through the cracks
Lies shall never be spoken in here
Tormented not by the heat of the sun
Even winter winds shall stay at bay
Recharged between these walls and your arms, each and every day
> *...sweet castaways safe from life's storms*

Finding the perfect spot between love and fire...
Lively palpitations jump from my chest
Only when into your eyes I do stare
Vertigo appears contagious in your presence
Entering willingly into our inseparable lover's lair
> *...that paradisaic balance keeping us warm*

Epiphany

Have you ever had a moment
An epiphany so to speak
Where the lasting memory
Of one single kiss
Caused your knees to wobble
Then become shockingly weak

Has there ever been an instant
Where flashing right before your eyes
The crystal clear vision of a beautiful woman
Left you silent, motionless, hypnotized

Do you recall a single minute
Where time seemed it could not pass
For the only thoughts forced from your brain
Were of that first perfectly formed hug
Wishing forever this embrace would last

Have you ever gone a complete hour
Sixty entire minutes of ticking time
Where you try to erase these memories away
Yet the attempts are always sublime

When was the last time
You suddenly awoke
Drowning within a puddle pool of sweat
Caused by the raging pounds within your heart
Of the woman whose kisses you can never forget

~continued~

I know,
Yes, I will honestly admit
Staring intently at the calendar upon the wall
Not one single day has ever passed
I do not place the check mark
Think of you
Then bawl

Silence Between the Sound

Once kneeling at love's mourning bench
Full of wisdom, no direction to be found
Only tasting the bitter bites of the apple
Not hearing the silence between all the sound

As mist descends, pain washes away
In this dreamlike state of mind
You walk upon me with a flowing glow
Appearing as Venus and Freya intertwined

Transforming my decadence to elegance
Ironing out all the rough spots you find
Stealing my breath with your total touch
Just placing your satin hand gently upon mine

Your promise is to love me in slow motion
So my heart can savor each anxious beat
Knowing that when it comes to mingling tongues
Our deeds of flesh make one another complete

For fear of the eternal haunting
Of an unfinished tender kiss from your lips
When with you my eyes shall never come closed
Not wanting to become blind to a vision that shatters
The possibility you are a dream that has been exposed

Once kneeling at love's mourning bench
Thinking true love a merit less deed
Then you dance me slowly to the music between the sound
I now realize your passionate love is a need I need

Warm Whispers

I think that I should tell you...
Taking in a moment of silent remembrance
Mind exploring snippets of memories past
You appeared out of nowhere like an apparition
Sharing a smile that left my heart beating hard and fast
   ...I thought about you today

We were holding hands in unknown destinations...
Within every word or sentence you have expressed
Each syllable carries a vibrant lilting melody
Your voice beholds the traits of the whitest of whites
Pure warm whispers floating without pain or debris
   ...the sound of your voice told me all was okay

I think that I should tell you...
Each gentle touch you lay upon my skin
Leaves me eternally compliant to your commands
It is as if your fingers have formed into bracelets
Loving shackles holding me for your most intimate of demands
   ...within your prison of passion I shall willingly remain

Using life's few moments of silence...
Tomorrow shall never just be another occurrence
The ink to our last page of history shall never become dry
Thoughts of last hugs and kisses are clear sacrilege
Everlasting love never knows not a yesterday
Where within the final act true lovers have said goodbye
   ...to smile at the precious memories we have obtained

Nana's Voice

Just because of you, she says
As the remembrance comes into fold
I could do the potty dance
When I was only two years old

You taught me many things of life
Alphabet affirmations was a game
Slugs and bugs were icky things
The alligators in the attic we would name

~continued~

You showed me the shape of my shadow
How to skip, three steps and a bounce
Dressing me up as your little cheerleader
My presence you would always announce

Funny how the years go by
We remember the little things
But on this day, I close my eyes
Your words I still hear sing

Come walk with me, you would say
In your loving nana's voice
Everything in life, you make yourself
You always have a choice

No conversations with strangers
It can hurt chasing wasps and bees
Sticks and stones hurt worse than words
Nature's lullaby sings to flowers like me

Never stop being rambunctious
Keep your child spirit intact
Always stop to smell the flowers
It is life's most important fact
Let your senses feast
As you take in their aroma each day
Know deep within your heart
Their fragrance
Keeps the attic's alligators at bay

Drift

Cool clear water
Drifting astray
Any destination
Just one notion away
Waves cresting slowly
Watching the dimming of the day
Reaching for paradise
Enjoying the ocean spray

Slow ride
Patience
No hurry
No gains
Just enjoying the view
No struggles
No strain

Freedom
Looking around aimlessly
Blue sky
Blue sea
Hastiness is taboo
From life's troubles
The mind can flee

Eyes closed
Feet up
Ten minutes per day
I sit
I dream
In the deep blue
All stressors of life
Just go drifting away

Procession

Morning rays of sharp cobalt blue
Vault through the dusty windowpane
Announcing it is time to cease the battle
A throbbing rage within the temporal vein

So it is this day as all the previous others
Out of addiction or habit I awaken alive
Starting a new dawn guilty only of innocence
Hoping all of life's scars and stitches disintegrate
Staying immune to the memories they contrive

As a stalled pedestrian upon a crowded sidewalk
The masses await a funeral procession to drive by
With no place to go and my clothes outlined in black
I felt it was time to learn how others said goodbye

The cold breath of the autumn morn
Helped expedite the movement of my feet
Sitting alone on the very last pew available
In case I needed to make a very quick retreat

I sat awaiting the inevitable
Kind words and loving songs from yesterdays
Yet the weary eyes of those chosen to speak
Orated of an eternal agony within their souls
How their absence left this dead man in dejected decay

One by one they tried to vindicate
The reasons they never stopped by to say hello
Through some form of elimination process
They felt being here at this moment
Became the absolute greatest gift they could bestow

~continued~

As they all marched out they hid their eyes
Their feelings of guilt will surely soon dissolve
They will all parachute back into their normal routines
Their forgetfulness of a friend now totally absolved

I could never walk out of this event consequence free
How could I be immune to this play's final act
Was I the only one to view this as some bizarre sacrifice
Should friendship not include some form of life-long pact

That night I stared intently upon the moon
Allowing my thoughts to float to those for whom I cared
The ones who caused me to shine a great smile
Those un-erasable grand memories that were shared

Pondering that on the other side of this planet
Tomorrow is already being disbursed
Having lived the life of a procrastinator
Can leave all friendships speeding in reverse

So at this moment I find the ambition
To transverse the miles behind these eyes
Reaching out to you my friend from long ago
To ensure we are bathed in a plethora of hellos
Before we must say that final goodbye

Ing…

Patiently waiting…

Wanting…
A spring shower soaked romance
An angel clad in a silken evening gown
Clinging crisply to her every voluptuous curve
As fragile drops of heaven come whispering down

Needing…
A love reminiscent of candy
An everlasting lifelong lemon drop
Emitting tartness to pucker up my buds at night
With a daylong sweetness that never stops

Wishing…
A diary of living dreams my quill composes
An open book of devotion with no chapter undone
Tales of wide smiles and the difference in me
Since the delirious symptoms of Cupid's disease have begun

Desiring…
A daily focus to never lose touch
An aspiration from your aura's glow
Both always singing a song to make love to
We just fit right with our ebb and flow

Lusting…
A self-imposed slavery to scintillating eyes
An unceasing desire for the beautifully obscene
Knowing together each day ends in a sacred night
Hungering to cause each other to emit primal screams

~continued~

Realizing…
A golden pathway has lain before us
An entrance should soon open free
Singing away all the hurt from before
Realizing this woman has always been a friend to me

    …and she blossomed

Kiss Me Please

Tangled joyously within your affection…
Knowing your heart is my smile's keepsake
A permanent pictured locket within my soul
You give me a comfortable feeling of pure energy
I have a thirst only your lips can console
          …your brilliant radiance articulates

The nervous prelude to a first kiss…
My fires now burn with open rampage
Vanity tells me there is nothing left to say
Just hoping my movements are not all fingers and thumbs
Please do not let fluttering monarchs get in our way
          …for this breath of life you tease me in wait

My hearts enslavement shall be revealed…
Discovering the energy in your soft whispers
Our vibes sense a special something on the horizon looms
Staring into your eyes of emerald green and cornflower blue
One taste of your lips and these tears will transform into blooms
          …knowing this pressing of lips shall be unique

Butterflies of equilibrium never lie…
Fears withering away at the thought of a trace
Of the lacquer of your lipstick drawing close to my face
Hidden passions now being fully expressed
Against my own, your luscious lips are now pressed
          …a kiss from my ivory rose has left me weak

I Shall Watch Every Sunset

I shall be released
I shall start again renewed
I shall walk with my head high
I shall not have my mind in a brood
I shall take joy in every day
I shall be sheltered from the storm
I shall watch my children grow
I shall promise to protect and keep them warm
I shall grow from my mistakes
I shall learn my lessons well
I shall smile at those who smile at me
I shall not live my life inside a shell
I shall be a man
I shall not dwell on love that is lost
I shall move myself forward
I shall not care about the cost
I shall be released
I shall take each day in stride
I shall watch every sunset
I shall not be denied

Cleansing

Stroll with me under a violet moon…
Shall we walk purposefully without hesitation
Yet in slow motion to savor scenery and time
Interlaced fingers display our coexistence circle
This forever passion aesthetically sublime
        …let us enter the forest of tomorrow's domain

My lady lay your body down…
Enslaved by your consuming intimacy
Rains penetrate the pores our now fiery flesh
Respiration now a difficult afterthought
As we kiss wildly in tongue tied mesh
        … find solace from a cleansing summer rain

Inhale the rapturous sweet breath…
Skin tingles from the scent of Euphoria
Strategically placed delicately upon your skin
My lips begging to taste of the neck once more
Your scent causes the arousal of the animal within
        …of washed oxygen and sweet pine

Listen intently to the symphony of life…
There is an arena of concealment within my chest
Four chambers once forming a motionless abyss
Then came an invisible invasion of emotional impulse
Kick-starting this heart with your very first kiss
        …as your heart beats in tune with mine

THE ICON

On an aimless jaunt across a deadened meadow
Wasting time following paw prints within fresh snow
Suddenly a large shadow fell upon my chosen path
Turning, I vision a large granite mausoleum upon a plateau

Trekking over as curiosity seizes the mind
Wondering what type of person may lie dormant inside
Mouth agape, staring at a pristinely kept monument
On the entranceway a wondrous calligraphy was inscribed

Here lie the bones of an icon
This building harbors his mortal being
Although bodily corrupted by the disease of time
His soul hovers around outside for those sightseeing

Left an orphan as the result of a twisting storm
Never allowing his pure heart to be caged
A pugilist with mighty words as well as fisticuffs
For the side of right he was always engaged

An interesting epitaph to cause the brain to spin
Thinking this would be someone worthy to meet
Sitting now, back pressed against the door
Time to watch the high new sun melt the snow
I reach into my backpack for a cold pop and something to eat

An unexpected attack of drowsiness
Caused me to momentarily close my eyes
Then by some freak transformation or osmosis
A large man from a distant time and place
Said "Nice to meet you" and was awaiting my reply

~continued~

He began telling his tale in voice strong and smooth
About a time where men met steel with steel
Where heroes stayed true to their path of glory
A moment in history where chivalry was still real

The tornado arrived on his family's Indian land cabin
Around the time he was the age of seven or eight
He alone buried his parents and a sister of two
Beyond his years in the brain capacity
Relinquishing all of life's events to a supreme fate

Alone for years in the wilderness
Surviving on his own kill, wild berries and nuts
Contorting within his young mind true destiny
Home is within the heart whose doors never shut

Spending many years playing make believe
Where only the wind knew of his name
Realizing through loneliness the value of company
When he finally does meet upon other human beings
He must always greet them with thunderous acclaim

At the age of twenty he knew it was time
To find a place in which to hang his hat
Stumbling into the first town within his path
He would neither leave, nor ever look back

Taking his first job as a glass washer
In the local watering hole
He told his tale to all who listened
Those singing sad drunken lullabies he would console

~continued~

25

As time moved on he made his mark
Becoming the Sheriff of this growing town
When times got rough, he remember his past
Being a long way from nowhere
With only loneliness and a constant frown

Some drown blues by lifting the brown bottle
Others through worship Sunday morning and night
He found life even-keeled and copasetic
By just making sure he was on the correct side of right

His legend was not just that of a fine god-fearing man
Nor because he fought criminals with his mighty brawn
It was because he never met a human that was not a friend
Each and every friend he would greet with a hug
Until all the feeling in your arms was gone

I could feel the sun begin to set
As the icons hazing existence faded away
He said his last words for me are written in stone
Read the back of his temple before I stray

Waking from this four hour nap
Shaking my head, wondering if it were real
Walking to the back of the temple of this man
As I read his words my tears were not concealed

Exist or else
Stay or drown
Live or vanish away
Think beyond the looking glass
If only for one single day

~continued~

Never take the leaving train
Always be happy to where you arrive
Love other humans as you would love yourself
If you truly wish to feel you are alive

As the night moved on
I strolled home with a smile
Eyes and heart opened by fate
Now once a year
I walk this path
To reread the icons last words
Releasing mind and body of all hate

You've Got the Power

Search beneath the beyond
Learn the lines in between
Let the candle burn
Reach beyond your furthest extremes

Do not hold that thought
Step loudly, shout and scream
Find respect for yourself
You are a tremendous human being

Get back in stride
No detours ahead
Let loose songs of exultation
As you bounce up from your bed

Let it all go
You are a rare find
Sign your name to the future today
Believe in your spirit, extraordinary ways
Put them all on display

Do not forget to remember
You are contagious this way
For your beauty is untouchable
When you take back the power of today

Wildflower

Independent
Free
Relinquished of care
Anyone can view
See your beauty unfold
Whether standing alone
Or with others sharing the same flair
I pass you by
On many a day
Not soaking you in

~continued~

Not hearing what you say
You are a reminder
That we can stand tall
No matter where our roots are planted
Enduring all seasons
Spring, summer, or fall
Seen many days
In fields
The side of the road
It is so easy to overlook
The beauty you bestow
Thank you for reminding me
Rules can be broken
A garden is not necessary
Wildflower has spoken

Changing Hues

Throw away your useless inventions
Let the interior odyssey take you away
Baptize yourself in laughter this morning
Change hues, it is a brand new day

Take all of your second chances
As the tears and years start rolling by
Today is a golden opportunity
For breath taking moments that make you sigh

Promise yourself to remember
The many splendors of the sun
Take a walk in the sounds of nature
Get caught in the act of having fun

Remove the rock from your heart space
Take in the lies of a lonely friend
Hang on to every word they utter
Your listening may help them mend

Response and responsibility
For this moment, ignore their call
Today is your ticket to the world
Rise up, be proud, stand tall

Tomorrow you can let your saga continue
Today, you are joining life's grand band
Dunk your mind into a healing pool
Take your own happiness by command

Today is a single-track seduction
Move your feet, get off your duff
Bathe in the dawn's early light
Doing nothing is not doing enough

Wind's Whisper

Trace elements of wind's breath
Carry your downy whispers over to me
Commencing this soul's instant regeneration
An antidote to all the day's course circuitry

Just the simplest of articulations
Flowing like liquid velvet from your lips
Wraps my heart with invisible chains
Causing pandemonium to the beats rhythm
Arteries feeling the abeyance, as I attempt to get a grip

These arms of mine become clingy
Your seraphic voice fills my every empty space
Even if only the softest of plumy whispers
You arouse me to a warm, cuddly embrace

Each time I sit alone casting lazy shadows
Your voice in absence by time and space
Hearing expirations from the whistling wind
The beautiful truth causes me to fall a little harder
You are whispering from a distance
So I can hear your loving grace

Nobody's Diary

As I was drowning
Within a fistful of sand
Amethyst tears fell from my eyes
I was reading nobody's diary
When our symmetry caused me to cry

Perspective
Signals and messages
Absorbed and swallowed from fresh ink
An account so lusterless
Yet shadowing my own
Nobody faded away in a blink

Was this a true healing vision
Or a decent into madness for show
Can nobody cause a quest for reality
Making me realize there is still time to grow

Calling an end to the ultimatum for ego
No umbrella for this cascade of tears
Nobody awoke me this very moment
Causing a quest of fire for my remaining years

Converging with all thirsty nobodies
Feeling burdened by the burning of time
Removing the swords from our once quiet mouths
Wave them with purpose, wildly in the air
Becoming righteous, inspiring the sublime

~continued~

Nobody's story need be foreboding
One can hope for a sanguine farewell
Dust off your dreams
Race with destiny now
Make somebody's story a difference
A chronicle of virtuousness worthy to tell

Sacred Wind

An old oaken bench and easel
Sit next to the bustling stream of crystal blue
A painting of the valley deck and mountains
Is placed for all whom pass by to easily view

The canvas proclaimed the peaceful beauty
A mental sequence of the scenery this very day
One's diary of dreams could begin in this very spot
Nature's sweet essence causing the mind to go astray

The locals state the old master painter
Arrives to hold court each day around noon
Happily spinning yards of yarns and fairy tales
Before he begins his oration of pending doom

~continued~

Making his entrance into the parking lot
In an ancient topless jeep to inhale fresh air
The painter waddled bow legged up to his perch
Sun stained skin offset the graying of his long hair

Standing upon what he claims his family perch
Where his father and father's father before him also painted
Announcing himself as Sacred Wind to the vast gathering crowd
Shaking callused rough hands with everyone to get acquainted

He began telling tales of his upbringing
In a log cabin not far away within the woods
Stating the walls are covered from ceiling to floor
With canvases showing the view from where we all stood

Orating loudly now as he stood proud and tall
Claiming one could easily read his history from his scars
Covering battles with bears, years of hard manual labor
And one he said was from a bar fight with smashing guitars

"It was over 92 years ago this very month
My great-grandfather first painted these lands
He told my father this was art of an endless creation
As he lovingly moved the horsehide brush in his hand"

Sacred Wind discussed the paintings within his home
How this very view had been altered over the years
Just as our very own flesh evolves into dust
His family's paintings show the erosion of his fears

Gritting his teeth, we could all sense a vapor trail
That would leave his mouth as he again started to speak
There were to be no perishing passions from this man
He cherished these lands from this valley to the highest of peaks

~continued~

36

"There were years we could watch an eagles feather fall
Now they have forced away by some man made beasts
Once there were times in the fall it was just the leaves and myself
Present day we must invite the exhaust from your cars to our feasts

I know I am selfish in this internal war
Claiming all of these lands to be mine
Yet to not share their beauty would be a travesty
If only all others would handle them as a shrine

The avarice of modern day man
Hurts Mother Nature beyond her flesh
Is it not enough that we topple her prideful tall trees
Then think dumping wastes and solvents will help her refresh "

The red reflection of raging headlights within his eyes
Slowly ebbed to gray as he let out a final shriek
This battle had been fought for so many a year
It had taken its toll on his mind and physique

Before he gathered up his belongings
The beautiful painting, the easel and chair
Turning to the crowd that had gathered today
Stating he had just a few more thoughts to share

"For it has become all I have never wanted
Seeing the beauty here erode within a painting each year
There is an eternal duality within each and every one of us
To conquer the mountains of our lives and persevere

Just remember as you travel through these lands
One must stroke Mother Nature for all to bloom
As any man would desire to embrace a woman's love
You must cherish all her beauty as if you were her bridegroom"

~continued~

Sacred Wind then wisped away
Off to his cabin within the trees
Tomorrow would bring upon him a new day
As he would set up his easel and painting for all to see

Sweet Surrender

Surrender to me
Your heart, soul, and mind
I promise to be gentle
Caring and kind

Relinquish to me
Your thoughts
What you feel
Your deepest, darkest secrets
I promise to conceal

Cede unto me
All of your passion
I will soak it all in
Use it up
No need to ration

Deliver to me
Your light, tender touch
Cause me great trembles
You I will reach out to clutch

Surrender to me
See it all the way through
I make a solemn promise
The sweetest surrender
Will come back to you

Pillow of Dreams

Allowing myself each and every night
The pleasure of one single solitary vice
To enter upon my downy pillow of dreams
Allowing its tender softness to relax and entice

The nostalgic harmonies of an angel's wings
Whisper softly of a long ago time and place
Healing me of this impassioned hunger
A craving for the idyllic unified embrace

It was upon this sericeous perch of rest
When a halo of love floated into my view
Drifting across the great divide of my heart
Through misty distance I knew at once it was you

Reaching higher and higher for you to heal
Blackened nightmares of lonely gallows of pain
You hovered above, pressed your lips firmly to mine
With the gentle touch of a sweet summer rain

Lying here with ease half asleep each night
Knowing before each dawn you shall return
Wearing your vibrant smile of strawberry sunrises
Along with your temple of skin for which I yearn

Until the thought of you upon my cushiony rest
I could not feel the delicate texture of the rose
Living within a kingdom of forgotten dreams
Hearing now the resplendent sounds
Two bodies uniting can delicately compose

~continued~

It was here upon this cushiony repose
Our skin storm caused a galvanic spark
To me you also avowed your eternal love
Discovering my soul with that wonderful remark

There are just some things a man holds sacred
Like dancing with destiny to the furthest extremes
Or dreaming that a lovely angel appears each night
Ready to cuddle upon his downy pillow of dreams

Catharsis

My headset often speaks to me
On a exceptional frequency
When searching for atonement
Aiding in litigating cerebral debris

So often times this holding cell
With all the ramparts inside my mind
Needs mellow reverberations
A simple groove to aid the unwind

A constant building gravitation
Of life's daily lies that bind
No struggle begets no progress
Internal decay and imbalance combine

Days spent amongst human ruins
Can leave one an aspiring sociopath
A victim of wandering lust
Or a parasite full of wrath

My headset gives me departure
A sanctuary when all souled out
Ridding myself of pride's paranoia
Killing the inertia within to shout

Within my headset's sanctuary
John Coltrane plays his horn for me
Miles Davis soothes this opaque beast
Dizzie Gillespie mirthfully helps me flee

This catharsis turns to surrender
Their instruments place me within their palms
Just hoping privacy does not attract a crowd
As I patiently work myself into a calm

Still Standing

Still standing
Weathered the storms
Wind blown and tattered
Unable to keep warm

Somehow still standing
After all of life's travails
Rustic in beauty
Held together
By rusted nails

Somehow withstanding
All the tests of time
I may be aging rapidly
Not quite aesthetic
As I was in my prime

Throw at me your winters
Your summer thunder strikes
I am still standing
Trying to make something of this life

Can you see the beauty
In something falling down
Holding oneself together
Not ready yet to drown

I am still standing
Everyone give me your best shots
You cannot put me down for good
I will not be forgot

Let Me

Orating to me benighted premonitions...
A once calming stream of devotion and trust
Now flows silently, not a ripple upon the emptiness
Your tenderness once raged like a maelstrom
Until your icon of flesh, dressed elegant in black
Refused to answer your calls of need and distress
    ...your soul has become a vile infernal abyss

All affections removed in an eternal tragedy...
So many choices of weapons to obliterate the beat
His twisted moralities left your heart pumping black
Baptizing you in the promises of future broken dreams
Never understanding his goal was to see you lost and broken
In order to deny you even the smallest of snacks
    ... your pin cushioned heart received a spider's kiss

Allow the sunshine of my tender embrace...
So here I stand with traces of integrity
Nothing like that past incredibly gorgeous man
My humility on parade for the world to view
But the shapes of true love I do understand
    ...to warm the frozen dusk of all your fright

Listen intently as the radio plays...
Help yourself to my pounding rhythms of life
Your darkened icon could never get this close
Allow me to show you the way back into love's light
Staring into my eyes to view the passionate center of me
As I touch you tenderly, handing you a snowy white rose
    ..."let me be your shelter from the endless night"

Mental Sun Screen

Sun shower beating down
Palms giving comforting shade
The colors of the wind flowing fluidly
Traveling from jasper to jade

Quixotic thoughts running rampant
The imagination envisions shiny things
The headset is just playing static
Yet I can still here Billie Holiday sing

Consolation in isolation
Practical insanity can prevail
When the aloha wind comes calling
Removing the dust and paper from ones sails

Give me this mental breath mint
Moments alone to count grains of sand
Not the ones in imprisoned by the hourglass
Give me unfiltered from Mother Nature to my hand

There are moments that reality
Needs a break from the seasons of life
Give me a sun stroked revelation project
To clear my mind, my body of strife

The wind whispers that she loves me
Billie sings to me in rhapsody blue
The sand drifts away uncountable
Yet it is precious moments like these
One can escape life's harsh reality,
breath, and drink a cold brew

A Party of One

Staring out this dusty window
A life separated only by thin glass
Losing touch with all reality
No chemical vacation to help this time pass

Projecting crimson anger
My cellophane persona acutely aware
A party of one has formed
We are currently not going anywhere

Can I clear this mental static
Defuse the dragon as some may say
Is life like kissing the lipless
Can I really choose to conquer this day

There must be so much more
Than to sleep, dream, and die
Her memory remains vividly intact
I saw sapphire pools within her eyes

Staring out the window
Feeling the burdensome undertow
Seeing where the dandelions meet the roses
Finding the power to stand and grow

Chewing up valuable time
Without a compass, hearing invisible chords
No catching the invisible butterfly
Without a dead or alive reward

Staring out, sly grin in hand
Guided by voices so unknown
My dearest torment is over
It is not a crime to be alone

Pretty Today

A magic moment in time
As you called out to me today
Sauntering over, batting your eyes
Pink dress in your hand on display

Your soft sweet voice articulating
"Daddy, Please help me with my dress"
"I want to look pretty today"
You do every day, I lovingly confess

A comb through your hair quickly
No shoes upon your feet
Through the grass, circles you run
Smiling, that childish, happiness smile
Just loving the feel of the sun

Silent steps your tiny feet make
As you cry out playing with glee
You stop, you turn, you come sit right down
Placing yourself upon my knee
At two years old you proclaim out loud
Get your camera daddy, please take a picture of me

This river of tears invitation
Had me springing inside steadfast
You posed, said cheese, with the silliest of grins
I clicked swiftly before the moment had passed

You are anything but ordinary
A blessing in life's storm
You make me wish for more yesterdays
You have been pretty, no beautiful
Since the exact moment you were born

Symbolic Love

Love is a matter of…
Dionysus attempted to swoon Aphrodite
Handing her ripened red apples by the score
Slicing each succulent fruit down the middle
Showing the feminine love and beauty of a vulva as its core
>   *…just one bite*

Love is a matter of…
Golden harp strings form a ladder
Connecting both the heavens and earth
Ascending one's heart to higher states of love
Leading to a paradise of spiritual rebirth
>   *…listening to the chords*

Love is a matter of…
Within my hands a ladybug flutters her wings
Each spot on her back one month before love rings true
Releasing her in hopes she will go whisper my name
Softly into the ear of the one whose heart I hold true
>   *…having faith*

Love is a matter of…
Gliding across light wind blown ripples
We view a swan while tenderly holding hands
Revealing to us all that is sincere and pure
The breath of spirit her beauty commands
>   *…moving with grace*

~continued~

Love is a matter of...
Standing strong and tall under the beating sun
Having the flexibility to bend with the strongest wind
Take the path towards enlightenment tracing my stems
Beyond all heavens our bamboo passions shall transcend
    ...moving to the sway

Love is a matter of...
Lakshimi was created from my grit and pearls
Venus rode atop me to sail to the shore
My hard casing may not always be a vision of beauty
But my shell is sometimes the protective quality,
Love sometimes yearns for in order to endure
    ...feeling secure

Love is a matter of...
Blooms fertilized by the blood of Adonis
See his burning passion for Aphrodite within this rose
It is sensual, sacred, and all things romantic
Handing it to you my love, to show my desire flows
    ...seeing true beauty

Night's Chimera

Bad dreams infesting my state of torpor
Enlightenment not a companion to the itch in my brain
She reigns my nights when the air becomes still
Untamed devastation in my charred emotions domain

Lying in wait for the darkest of night
This chimera has taken my karma her slave
With her comes a song of crawling jagged bones
Accompanied by a chorus of screams from the grave

Scent explosions of burning black licorice
A companion to her acrimonious tongue
Bleeding my disease with ghastly fantasies
Pleasures of the flesh that have been left unsung

This beast orates in dark scaled circles
Shrieks conform to be louder than words
Whaling I shall forever burn in the morrow
For lies long since forgotten,
Bloodlettings that previously occurred

Representing the ghosts that haunt my past
Highlights of my failures she triumphantly extols
No medication can remove the black storms of her eyes
As she performs a total eclipse of a once vibrant soul

Fading out
The carnage done
Leaving a frozen heart engraved in black
The rising sun mists my dark stalker away
If I refuse to sleep can she come back?

~continued~

Finding joy within the dawn's emptiness
Yet the sticky residue of raw evil still haunts
I have a disease where my wrongs become bad dreams
Visiting me with Satan's creatures each night to taunt

This Molotov concoction I call my mind
Desires the morning to bring my true redeemer back
One that allows me to smell the roses in full bloom
To forgive me when my sinister side gets me off track

Tempest

Time's arrow has lost its feathers...
Shall I be the feast for your body's famine
The fruit at the bottom of your sensual parfait
Is my name the echo of your every breath
To my heartbeat's anthem will you forever sway
            ...the nock has fallen free

Please do not calm this storm...
Sensing your coquettish manipulations
Seeing fervent lust intense within your eyes
The sexy tightening of your nightshirt
As your stiff apple blossoms fall and rise
            ...it is the greatest escape for me

Together we find satisfaction...
Hair flowing on fancy satin pillows
Licking your luscious lips to drive me insane
I am the lover to cure your inner beast
Turning on some sultry Barry White
While handing you a chilled glass of champagne
            ...just letting the disc repeat

You are the shelter for every evening...
As our elastic limbs grip, slip, and tangle
Hands of lust keeping our skin purified
Feeling no air between fingers and flesh
It is almost uneasy how good this feels
The internal tempest our passion provides
            ...twined as one as our bodies meet

Just Dreaming…

Strolling mirthfully through the mist…
Cerebral turbulence brought on by love's fever
She appears swiftly, soaring without wings
Thinking angels were on the verge of distinction
Entering euphoniously to the strum of golden harp strings
        …within this chaotically dreaming mind

Cardinal daisies braided within her hair…
A single glimpse brings instant gratification
Accuracy requested for this flawless view
The epicenter of everything precious and pure
Just to touch the beauty of her skin seems taboo
        …the absolute vision of beauty defined

Tempting the dance of forbidden tunes…
Dancing slowly with tears in my eyes
A never-ending love song amorously plays
Tingles from your touch ignite every part of me
In your arms the grayest of days drift away
        …causing me to sway to their tribal beats

Stealing the still of my nights away…
There shall be no evidence of wasted ink
Recording these resplendent night visions a must
Awakening each day with a quill full of thoughts
This writer's heart sprinkled with your angel dust
        …an affair of our dreams, sweet and discrete

…about a girl

Inked

You have inked my soul
With the most permanent of tattoos
It's watercolor lines
The most vibrant of hues

Upon your engraving
Lies clarity's essence
A love free and clear
Memories as presents

Coated in many colors
Where this impression lies
A colorful rainbow was born
From your glow, your smile
Your scintillating eyes

You have inked my soul
Forever, not just today
A place of peace and harmony
A haven permanently stored away

Within your etching
Perpetual passion echoes
Blended with the summer breeze
And the scent of a blooming red rose

You have inked my soul
With an icon for all time
My soul can now be called heaven
It says your smile is now mine

Guinevere

Subtle movements of a visionary
Attempting to find a sense of place
As a subtle handful of quietness
Brushes gently across my face

It was the onset of autumn
A place of enchantment, sitting calm
When a spectrum of violet passed me
Sparkling like dewdrops on the morning lawn

Shimmering wings aflutter
Crystal echoes from across the pond
A celestial descent into a delicate dance
My cloud of unknowing on how to respond
Bathed in dawns liquid indigo
She had the appearance of dancing swans
Finding myself closer to center
In her reverence I was a pawn

Was this the call of a siren
Crystal echoes as she spoke
Her breath was a healing mist
What inspired effect would she provoke

A hundred blooms flew from the ground
Landing delicately within her hair
The crickets chirped a song of serenity
A circle of warmth suddenly filled the air

~continued~

This angel solved the algebra of beauty
Spirit and form no trick of light
I began my surrendering process
There was communion in her eyes of white

For want of her I begin to move
A liaison of love about to spawn
Reaching out for her hands of silk
I blink and she is gone

A sentiment of knowing overcomes me
Her flight of fancy a visionary crime
Leaving echoes in my void
I could not have seen an angel today
Being simply a citizen of time

The Gravedigger

Vibrations pound frantically upon the thin tin roof
A symphony announcing the potency of the storm
Among mortals this world forever fades to gray
Pondering if life has value +before one is born

Charred abhorrent dementia of yesterday's ghosts
Benighted shadows soap and water still hold close
Dark memories past cannot be scrubbed or cleansed
Out of his own spirits the gravedigger now seeks amends

No longer able to separate the once radiant prisms
Of each of his placement's paling chromosomal hue
Sensing only darkness from the ashes upon their eyes
Awaiting earth's buried creatures are starving to chew

Once able to handle the madness of living's streets
Making fun of those always swallowing their swords
Then on that day underneath his colorful beating heart
He sensed an apparition his soul could not absorb

Images from the past consumed his being
Feeling the urge to rip open this casket of oak
Unlike all days past he just moved freshly churned earth
Never imagining his zest for life would be provoked

Standing alone in this monumental field of color
Flowers of love surrounding every headstone in sight
Never thinking his profession had regards to himself
Until this moment when life and pain decided to unite

~continued~

Upon her left hand was a glistening golden ring
Sparkling diamonds winked vibrant from morning dew
Gasping for breath, sprinting frantically away
Remembrance of the day she had whispered I do

Storm raining down hard inside the shanty tin room
The gravedigger's history ran frantic through his mind
Retrieving visions of the day he could hear her breathe in
Prior to the days he allowed golden treasures to rob his love blind

Once when he was on bended knee
Handing her the crowned jewel upon her hand
Proud that he presented love hidden in wealth
Yet, she only wished for his affection upon command

Through all the years that had long since passed
This man stayed solemn to make his amends
Learning she had later found a humble man to love
One who did not relish in the amounts he could spend

Rolling scenes of lasts entered within his mind
Last kisses
Last laughs
Last dance
Last words of begging for just one more day
Asking for the opportunity to again prove his love
And love said no,
you have already wasted your last chance away

Knowing now, today, his penance was paid
For allowing his true love to pass frivolously by
The gravedigger knelt down
Placing calloused hands upon his own face
Producing the final tears that he ever would cry

Mornin Sunshine

Finding my morning contentment
Staring out this window slightly ajar
Taking in the scents nature's mother has to offer
Ears now piqued to the soft rhythmic sounds
Of a neighbor strumming Jim Croce on the acoustic guitar

Matured to the substance of love's pure existence
Ever since the day you brought absolution to my mind
Blue days have faded silently far into the distance
Like old hole filled jeans one wears each day to unwind

Standing here ready to worship the memory
Of the day our bodies combine into a single silhouette
Just sing out my name into a southerly breeze
Soon I will be there to perform our heartfelt duet

When you see my arms whaling about frantically
Please note I am not simply waving a wild hello
I am blissfully drowning in the sea that is your eyes
Over taken by the waves of your smile's effervescent glow

There is no stopping this jubilant gaze out the window
Knowing you are staring at the exact same blue sky
Smiling at the thought of sacred nights of the future
Pouring my heart a glass of your liquid sunshine
I stare in awe at your photo, releasing a great big sigh

Unspoken Words

I've wept for the last time
My tears have gone dry
With the greatest of shames
Why must you say goodbye

Memories linger
Of that last dark embrace
Tears of envy
Flowed down my face

Words were unspoken
Cold roses on the ground
The shadow of your stranger
New love you had found

Do not blanket me in comfort
You will find no afterglow
Your words smashed in to me
As I watch you turn and go

Delusional acceptance
The distance surfacing ahead
A very long walk home
To a cold and empty bed

Thirsting for your therapy
A sip is all I need
Thunder in the distance
You walked away
I bleed

Nature's Blend

Mountain scenery
Emits just the right sound
No ears required to listen
Just eyes open wide, wandering around

The world of tomorrow
Should listen to the calm
Cast its light of the future
Within Mother Nature's palm

This kind of happiness
Unconditional sensual bliss
Nothing left to be desired
Just the time to reminisce

~continued~

Do not take from me this perceived weakness
This gentle, tender, sensitive side
Give me wildflowers while I am living
Let the colors blend and collide

Nature shares a song
Lyrics pure, crisp and clean
Crying out to let the rest of the world go by
Enjoy the blooms, the greenery, and air so pristine

Memento

I have found my memento
Through a slow emotion replay
Pressing the click and repeat
No more wounds get in the way

Speech bubbles stymied
The pulse of my future beats
My memento is not candied cigarettes
Nor any chocolate covered sweets

I need not trinkets
Nor booty laden with gold
My memento is like the perfect brushstroke
A Picasso as your smile's glow slowly unfolds

Stargazing the sparkle
The constellations floating in your eyes
Escaping life's fishbowl within them
The glistening fluids keep me baptized

Everything never said aloud
Pours from the smile within your eyes
Hyper saturated beauty screams out
True happiness this way lies

I have found my memento
Leading me onward to a tenderness place
This treasure of all lifetimes
Is simply, the smile upon your face

Eyes Cannot Lie

Shining brightly throughout the night...
Swinging slowly, gently holding hands
The sun is setting as the moon takes command
You might hide your thoughts with twisting words
Your body language you think can alter the sway
But on this fantastic night, your eyes have given you away
    ...a touch of fragility seeps from the glow

Consuming fire is calling from your orbs of grace...
Softly stroking the tender skin upon your arms
Yes, you are falling for my gentle neck kissing charms
Staring deeply into your aroused eyes now ablaze
Both of us feeling a moment so special we do not dare blink
Am I dreaming in splendor or ardently on eternity's brink
    ...passions illuminating the desires within you that grow

Within the elegance your declaration is made...
Both eyes gleam upon me with a radiant caress
Causing me to scream with elation "I must confess"
Take my hand, deliver me, please see all of me as you touch and feel
But please take your time my angel, for this all appears so surreal"
    ...spoken only with a committed look of needs

Beneath the fire filled eyes of a woman in love...
Once wild at heart until your love I felt
Now just open your eyes and watch this man melt
You breathe, I sigh, bringing with it an inner piece
So on these clearest of nights
When the sun is setting
The moon shining high above
I see stars twinkling within your eyes
They tell me not only of your fire for me
But also you have given me all of your love
    ...is where the breath of eternity allows the embers feed

This Moment

Let us hold a sacred ceremony
Within the flickering of candle light
Becoming one with our inner beasts
Taste of the taboo with candied delight

For these brief moments shared together
We shall not be enslaved to life's bitterness
In these moments of silence let us observe
The mind seduction of a passionate kiss

When the mundane of day to day existence
Leaves innocence marred with a large black eye
These moments together in perfect harmony
Cause screaming heartbeats to euphorically revive

Tomorrow we may face the executioner
Slice our souls on the employment guillotine
But these moments we have now together
Sugar coats the sour of the daily routine

Sitting before you the mind clears all turmoil
Washing away everything said we did not mean
As we hold each others quivering flesh in enshrinement
This shuddering passion wipes yesterday's slate clean

Humiliations transcend into divine dignities
As we crawl into the elysian fields of each others arms
Knowing this touching washes away all the ugliness inside
For this moment, together, nothing can do us any harm

The Promise

The antique glider rocker now silently still
Jake's newborn son tucked into the nearby bassinet
The first-time father beams a rainbow aura of elation
Gently opening an eroded old King Edward cigar box
Full of long ago memories he promised to never forget

Staring down at the week old slumbering smile
Daydreaming of days, weeks and years ahead
Thankful to be alive, to share in this wondrous joy
Now remembering when he himself were born
On the very day they received a form letter
Jake's father would finally return home from Vietnam
Within a body bag because he had been shot dead

The first item removed for this practice show and tell
Promising to share it often over his sons growing years
Taking out the purple medal shaped like a heart
Pinning it upon the side of the bassinet
Doing his best to hold back a fountain of tears

Carefully opening a letter from his father's best friend
To this day he is remembered as granddaddy Dale
Dale had been there with his father until the bitter end
With a promise of his own he must now fulfill
Telling this young man in a thirty-six page letter
Marvelous tales of his father in pinpoint detail

This letter ended with the gory details
Of how within his father's arms Dale bled
Injured he carried Dale to the boundary of safety
Until a lone sniper's fire shot his daddy dead

~continued~

Holding a picture up for his son to now see
Showing Dale and his daddy in uniforms of full dress
Both handsome young men, smiling, in a whimsical way
Enjoying a moment of leave away from the war's stress

Jake's mind now wondering to a time long ago
Adolescent summers spent on Granddaddy Dale's farm
Removing his old wood whittling pocket knife from the box
Reminiscing about nights spent learning all of Dale's charms

Jake now thought of every month of June and July
From the age of three until he was a ripe old sixteen
Learning the values of hard work and so much more from this man
Always looking forward to his summer routine

As darkness descended upon each hot Oklahoma summer day
After the crops had been tended and tools put away
They would sit upon the porch, Dale in the very rocking chair
That Jake and his son this evening did sway

A pile of wood sat next to the chairs
Each night they each would grab a choice piece
As they shaved and formed animals with their special knives
Dale would start spouting words of wisdom
And often times it seemed he would never cease

Jake now pulled out a small journal
Each night before bed he would jot down Dale's spurts
For he knew there would come a day he would be a father
Knowing full well Dale's words of advice could never hurt

~continued~

"It is okay to experiment with failure
That way there are no mixed messages when you succeed
If you find a cause that brings your internal fires to a burn
Do not make token gestures
Keep fighting until you bleed"

Jake thumbed through his journal for more whittling wisdom
"Never allow evil ones to kill your consciousness
They just wish to parade it about like a souvenir
Keep things simple, like just telling the truth
If you promise tomorrow tonight, you must be sincere"

Jake now pulled a fishing bobber from his box of gold
Large grins now spread widely across his face
Daleism's said you had to always fish in the morning
Starting the day putting those lil suckers into their place

Six days a week, from the first of June until July's end
Dale would awaken Jake long before the sun's dawn
Claiming it was important to always get the day's first glimpse
Of God's planetarium before all of our day's become gone

Daleisms were not limited to whittling
He shared them while fishing and walking as well
Recalling he once said wisdom floats just like your bobber
When someone tries to drown out your wisdom
Within a jealous house that person must dwell
"Of all the things you throw away
Never get rid of your chosen mourning star
Within it you can find perfection within your pain
Until your rite of sunrise sandpapers over your scar"

~continued~

As Jake read these items to his beautiful son
He could smell the farm's waving wheat
Tingles flowed up and down his body
Remembering hard work, sweat, and the heat

Telling his son there is much more to learn
But for this day I will share only a few more
We will have many days and more nights together
To share in Granddaddy Dale's loving lore

While walking back one day in a sprinkle of rain
Jake remembered hearing granddaddy state,
"Live your life between the rainbows ends
Enjoy the spectrum of colors within the pouring rain
Chasing the gold is only for silly Texan fools
Never finding it's intent is to drive you insane.

When you feel that your life is swimming in circles
Counterclockwise to a school of hungry sharks
Remember the one thing that you truly love the most
Your escape comes synchronizing this thought with your heart"

As a young man Jake devoured this knowledge
Knowing in his future these words would all make sense
It happened in the summer when he was only seventeen
Granddaddy Dale had died, but with a smile on his face
He had kept his promise
From the days he fought for his country's defense

~continued~

Jake was now holding his son tightly
Swaying slowly while humming the Ballad of the Green Berets
Whispering into his son's ear one more snippet of wisdom
It is the epitaph on Dale's headstone
To be read for forever, and a few more days

"For Dale clocks and calendars hold no value
We live on this earth completely incomplete
The truest future begins with our rising
So do not bow your head here in sorrow
On the other side of the clouds we shall meet"

Dale was one to always get the last word
So on the other side of the stone at his bequest
"If upon my stone you wish to leave graffiti
Please make it only of the verbal kind
One day this stone will crumble and fall
But spoken words are carried upon the wind
Always available to an open mind"

As Time Goes By (Miss You, Mom)

Just for this single solitary moment
Please, allow us to travel back in time
To inhale the smell of your spaghetti sauce
Mixed with oregano, your love, and thyme

Would it be remotely possible
If only just for this one night
We could once again view your insatiable smile
Throwing in lots of hugs so nice and tight

We have now passed another winter's shadow
Without your glow to warm our chilled insides
You were always a talented deep soul diver
Knowing when to comfort and when to guide

So it is each year as spring arrives
When the roses come into bloom
A Sunday holiday leaves a void in our hearts
You were the only one able to fill that room

Here we stand on a rainy morn
Your grandchildren with roses to share
They picked them fresh from our own back yard
To honor the memory of your tender loving care

As time goes by
The pain subsides
Loving memories viewed through crystal tears
Yet just for one single, solitary moment
We all wish we could hear your vibrant laughter
Echoing within our souls joyously loud and clear

Pieces

Falling to pieces
Again
Here I go
No one to share
No feelings to bestow
Sun coming down
On a hot blistery day
Falling to pieces
Again
My own heart I betray
Self-Doubt
Confidence
Ego all in check
Here I go once again
Falling to pieces
Trying to avoid this train wreck
Exiled to heartache
Underlying depression overcomes
Falling to pieces
I am a man
Not what I have become
What is the meaning
Of this loneliness renewed
Here I am again
Falling to pieces
Dreams left
Un-pursued
Burning ground below me
Enlightenment
Nowhere near

~continued~

Falling to pieces
Yet again
Pain unwilling to disappear
This man must struggle
Contemplation
No sleep
I simply fall to pieces
As I lie alone and weep

Beliefs

What makes this man
What are his beliefs
What is his creed
What causes him grief

I believe in the kiss
The passion
The lust
I believe in great friends
Honesty
Those you can trust

I believe in parenting
It is life's greatest gift
To help mold the future
To give little minds a lift

I believe in offering
More than one chance
I believe in the music
The beat, the dance

I believe in books
Movies and song
I believe that using our minds
Makes our heart and soul strong

I believe in the hug
The simple embrace
That shows that you care
Putting a smile on another's face

~continued~

I believe in humor
Making others laugh
I believe those who do not smile
Cut their life spans in half

I believe in flowers
Roses in bloom
I believe in chocolate
I love to consume

I believe that writing
Something each day
Keeps the minds evil spirits
The demons away

I believe there are powers
We cannot control
I believe in fairy tales
With ogre's and trolls

My creed is quite simple
To be loved you must give
You must do unto others great things
To continue to live

Muse

My vision appears in division
Seeing through tinted glass
Heart undermined
From the beauty of you
Hoping this feeling never shall pass

I awaken each morning
Within this place I know
It is raining within my eyes
Seeing your smile, the sheen upon every pearl
Causing underwater moonlight to arise

I never heard music
Until I saw your grace
To sunshine, I always seemed blind
But there came a day, I had nothing left to lose
Staring into your face, I found the definition of kind

Your laughter, like candy to my ears
Your eyes, my light while dreaming of romance
Your friendship, the air within my fairy tale land
Your smile, leaves me within a trance

When I hear your voice
It has a calming effect
Similar to a symphony of whales
The spell it casts, the power it holds
Keeps my soul willingly within your jails

~continued~

I could be within your arms
A long way from anywhere
Leaving everything sad far behind
A passage of life, a dream of a chance
Even if tonight it is only within my mind

It is a beautiful mess
When I think of you
Knowing one day I would be on a knee
Knowing I have your love, your friendship as well
How can anything be bothering me

Celestial Nomad

I am a celestial nomad
In a chromatic fantasy
Please, join my caravan
Bring the nearness of you to me
Let us start another journey
Travel daily all through time
Searching for the beauty in sadness
Positive energy of words that rhyme

Let us visit places and spaces
Deep within our minds
Full of love and spirit
Let no prejudices color our lines
Shall we search out bold conceptions
Look beyond the invisible seams
Taste strange fruit
Right off the vine
Break the silence of parallel dreams

Inspirational information
Shapes and patterns
Longing to be found
As we take this lifelong journey
Let our minds never be relaxed or content
To the language of love our tongues are bound

Come with me your nomad
All knowledge let us consume
Let us become one with all music
The beats, the rhythm, the tune
Let our journey make a difference
As we travel on our way
May it last a lifetime or two
As we make the world more beautiful each day

Frozen in Time

Should we enter a new ice age...
So many believe that love's prophecy
Calls for massive destruction before being rebuilt
Diagnosing this transitional phase between the two
Tans the heart's future and washes away any past guilt
     ...all life snared within a frozen embrace

The marrow of every creature's bones...
At first I thought you had a case of mistaken identity
Stating all of my thirsting desires you wished to quench
Finding life within the dust of those three little words
Although I am certain they sound much prettier in French
     ...motionlessly preserving love as time is erased

~continued~

A gathering of memories vanish…
All souvenirs and photographs
Erode from eternal winter's firm grasp
Yet the enchanting memories of a love beating pure
Allows two shining souls to endlessly clasp
        …within the silence without a trace

Tears of joy form an unmoving waterfall's interior…
The storm leaves no time for regression of past lives
No moments for last laments to wash away shame
At the moment of impact, with no seconds to spare
I breathed in the memory of what made life worthwhile
As my final act I smiled and rapturously shouted out your name
        …My last thoughts were of your beautiful face

Strum

No combination of the alphabet...
Feeling gently sentimental
Releasing my thoughts passive restraints
Attempting to find the moment's momentum
To tell you of my love with no constraints
　　...can reveal these feelings inside

Ever flowing rhythmic emotion...
Tingling all over like a giddy teenager
I cannot keep this adolescence repressed
On one knee I shall sing you a foolish lullaby
Of how your attention's became my quest
　　...a beating inside my soul now resides

You have become the harvester...
Ever since you introduced your mercy
I can now hear the morning birds sing
From the breaking of dawn's brilliant light
Until we cuddle watching the sunset in our swing
　　...of all life's beauty to which I cling

A shield against all sorrows...
Spirited summoning of common devotion
The easy tears of love cause no pain
Asking you a simple lover's question
Would you dance naked with me in the rain
　　...you strum the ballad of my heart's strings

Curves of the Future

Curves of the future
Waiting for the angel residing here
A never empty bottle of sunshine
One tiny piece of paradise
To be held close and dear

View the inner treasure
As one will soon form two
On the verge of a miracle
From this body's current perfect beauty
An angel will make her debut

Cast your cares toward her
Shared visions time will bring
Inhabit each others spirit
This angel is arriving
Feed her a book of dreams

Curves of the future
Drawing the eye near
A body with an afterglow
Consciously believing
There could be no greater beauty
Viewed within a mirror

Held in one still photograph
All that is beautiful to the human eye
Curves of a future angel
A nine-month journey of the heart
With a lifetime of love in reserve to supply

Serenade

Getting lost in words of chivalry
This poor man's Shangri La
Is it an artificial intelligence
Or some subtle non-macho flaw

Capturing the moment
The spirit of another age
Where troubadours and jugglers
Could confound the brightest sage

Most today have never sung a love song
Serenading to their sweetheart, guitar in hand
Proclaiming, YES, your love is supreme
Today they all hide within the band

Give me the days
With gallantry beaming
Filled with spirit and lore
Acquiring loves taste
The sacrament of the vine
True devotion of days of yore

Soften my heart
With the evolution of the art
The swooning of a damsel worthy of care
Men change your perspective
There is still a chance to change
Make courtship a gallant affair

A lunatic or poet
Is what I must be
To think that today's men are simply amiss
They find chivalry a strange illusion
Not understand the romantic power
Of a soft, sweet, serenaded kiss

Gladiator

Within the comforts of my madness
My mind takes journeys to undying lands
Envisioning myself a Provacator in the arena
A glistening gladius held firmly within my hands

Or maybe my role is that of a Secutor
A pursuer of the grand coliseum's roar
The women drooling at my subligaculum
My bronzed sica honed for the battles gore

Must we fight blind as the Andabatae
Delusions of invincibility make us deranged
The gladiators battled for their lives daily
Dark fields of pain have made little change

A pair of blue jeans forced on each morning
With glory, we pull them up as our greave
Or possibly donning a paisley printed necktie
Is the same as placing a galerus upon our sleeve

There can be no mistaken identity
We all have the scars of a daily war as our glue
Searching to find the void inside our own darkness
To encounter whatever it is which makes us true

Whether tackling our opponent as the Meridiani
Suffering through the grind from nine to five
We come to battle as the Dimacheri
With two swords to keep the family alive

~continued~

The ancient warriors hold no trademark
The realm of life's torment survived
Getting lost in our daily deliverance
The price of bread and deeds is not contrived

Longing to be glamorous as the Essedarri
Combating from chariots covered in gold
With enough willpower to keep us dead enough to live
With a mask of sanity as today's modern battles unfold

Glossary

Weapons of the Gladiator

galerus: metal shoulder piece
gladius: sword
hasta: lance
sica: curved scimitar
subligaculum: loin cloth

Types of Gladiators

Dimacheri fought with two swords
Essedarii fought from chariots like the Gauls and Britons
Meridiani fought in the middle of the day, after the wild beast fights
They were lightly armed
Provocator was armed like the Samnite with a *parma* and a *hasta*, his opponent was often the Myrmillo
The **Secutor** carried a large oval or rectangular shield, an *ocrea* on his left leg, a round or high-visored helmet, *manicae* at the elbow and wrists, and a sword or dagger

The Answer

There may be no chills to an evening
If it is your grace by which I stand
Warmed over by this cerebral inebriation
Just knowing, a day will come you make me your man

Ensnared deep within my veins
Dilated, they flow with confectionery stock
Pulsating all senses with your sweetness
No traces of acidic elements left to unblock

This love an endless journey
Unbridled aspirations within a dream
Pouring drops of primitive passion
Through my torrid, now sugared aortic stream

Asking a question with promise and threat
For whom do I see with eyes wide shut
Receiving good morning beautiful hugs in my view
Who is it that makes thoughts of tomorrow wonderful
Whose kisses leave me leave sugared, yet aflame
The answer, quite simply, it is you

The Little Things

The things that make you beautiful
Not all are for the eye to see
Your physical beauty is obvious
Like the flash of a firefly
Flaming red amongst giant trees

The things that make you darling
Are like chasing shadows upon the wind
Your sweet out of control laughter
Causing hearts to sing and ascend

The things that make you special
Which bring about a spark
To my faded blue eyes
Deep qualities of giving and mercy
You would tend to a broken butterfly

The things that make me crave you
Like a nightly narcotic prayer
Are not your glowing eyes
Or you wavy wind blown hair

The things that make you desirous
What gives my soul a lift
Is knowing deep with in my heart
Your presence is a gift

The thing that makes me love you
Something I would place on any marquee
You have this innate ability
To bring out the very best in me

Let Love Explode

Dark was the night
Cold was the ground
It was the autumn of life
Yet no one else is around

During a soul conversation
A spurious glory came to mind
Let us bring back romance
The most passionate kind

Under the same sky
With this moonlit serenade
Lover's bicker and squabble
Through relationship masquerades

Why can they not decipher
That there is no master code
Just keep reaching out together
You have just one lifetime
Let love explode

The remainder of the day spent wandering
Thoughts crowding my goose pimpled skin
This enigma of absolution
Was dulling the barbed wire within

Reach out, yell, share these thoughts
Lovers should fill their hearts with spring
Not stand in the dark shadows alone
Watching others happily dance and sing

~continued~

Touch her while your dancing
Kiss her softly upon the neck
Hand to her a bright red rose
Be old school, pick up the check

Hold her hand under a glorious sunset
Listen intently while she speaks
Tell her your inner most secrets
That her beauty causes your tears to leak

Behind closed doors
Find comfort there
Fulfilling her every need
In a faded breath, whisper in her ear
To her exquisite body you do now cede

Let her know, for want of her
You gave up your heart and soul
Placing them firmly within in her hand
Tell her home does not have to be
Where all the heartache lies
If of romance you take command

We may as well be strangers
I say to all those passing by
But please, listen intently
Save love, give romance a try

Spirited Colors

Colors cry out the spirit
Vivacious
Shiny in hue
What color
Do others see
When they are staring at you

Do you emit a spirited aura
Are you pastel
Bright and brilliant
Or do you give off shades of gray
Dull and no so vibrant

When you sleep
Are your dreams impressive
Colorful through and through
Or are they dark and lonely
Not really worth the view

What color do you give off today
Will others stare in awe
Do your colors cause the masses
To see reverence instead of flaw

Our colors tell our spirit
No need to be dense or bland
What color will you show today
Expressing your mood is grand

Through Picnic Dreams

The glistening brightness of a fairy tale...
This magnificent obsession of mine
I wear like a tattooed badge of pride
It is the splendor of my giant pounding heartbeat
When the shadows of our lips collide
>   *...florescent sunshine the marrow warms*

Treacly summer wine and softened chocolate...
Through barricades and stone covered walls
I would bound for the healing powers of your lips
You intoxicate me with a love of another kind
Making it difficult to just take slow gentle sips
>   *...cause erotic endorphins to excitedly perform*

Sweetly saturated I totally surrender...
Together through the seasons we have moved
Like hot breath passing through a fog that chilled
Dreaming of a reality that there will come a day
That all our future memories will be fulfilled
>   *...to the radiant translucence of your eyes*

My veins now open for euphoric bliss...
Once a total ball of confusion
Looking to fill all the spaces in between
Then she gave me just one kiss goodnight
Causing all thoughts and tears to have meaning
>   *...your love is not only a gift, but the prize*

If I Should Ever

If ever I should break your heart
Leave you crying
Sad
Or blue
Just remember
That I love you dearly
I am a better person
Simply
Because of you

If ever I should do such things
Stupid
Moronic
In your view
Recall
Please once again
I am human
But my heart is true

If ever you should awake one day
Wondering
If I am fine
Or feeling sad
Just retrieve your memory bank
Think of the past
Special times that we had

~continued~

If ever I should make you bawl
Cause you distress
Or pain
Please take just
One step back
Clear your mind
Let me try and explain

If ever I should make you cry
I apologize right now
Making mistakes is part of life
I have made them recently
Will again soon I am sure
Not always on purpose though
I am human
I learn and mature

Just a simple warning sign
If ever I should make you cry
It is never with a purpose in mind
I could not be that way
It would also bring tears to my eyes

Walk Alone

Big plans with an empty wallet
Midnight promises spewed on the fly
Offering drunken sentiments without any reason
Shiny porcelain words between the hi and goodbye

Orally torturing all who enter
Into the barflies spit splattering domain
Tales of sports, bad sex and food
The only cold comfort that remains

Unfortunately many here find his connection
This testimony to a paragraph of wasted life
Giving all who listen a pointless education
On the morose litigation of daily strife

Through bottomless seas of countless shot glasses
The emptiness of life's lead weight remains
There are no promises to be given
No guarantees within the sharing of names

Never feeling the bang of motivation's boomerang
We find the barfly a suffocating sight
His only hope the liquor will make him sweeter
So a lonely woman will bed him this night

Living each day within the empty
This cultural majority the generic norm
Wallowing in the pain of bleeding hearts
Only finding a broken rainbow after each storm

Sitting high upon his mountain top
Raising a toast from his barstool throne
A vision of death by drink in primetime
Some people are just destined to walk this earth alone

One Hard Winter

During those times I appeared withered and weak…
The coldest winter purloined my heart's sunshine
Removing my leaves, life no longer had a vibrant hue
The dark aspects of spirits caused me to feel the blade
Eviscerating all remembrances of things held dear and true
    …unfolding sorrow could not give me the strength to endure

It was during this time you started wishing me away…
Constantly fighting off those forever changing winds
The body crumbled as you attempted to cast me aside
Mental pollution permitted me to only write with blue ink
Watching the blue rose of my mood wither away, I cried
    …viewing me as transparent with no leaves remaining to assure

~continued~

My limbs sing a duet with the siren wind...
Once strong enough to down all my sorrow straight
Never emitting a shadowed melancholy portrait of despair
Have mercy on me I had always been the tower of strength
My begging bowl is now full as I cry out for you to share
    ...a ballad of how hard winters can lead one astray

Upon those days that you wish me away...
A broken rainbow once began at my roots
Its colors running, causing me to drown
The spring of life has arrived to connect its vivid colors
Aiding to keep burning tears from flowing down
So if you do not mind
You shall have to wish me away again every tomorrow
As the season brought back my greens from these horrid browns
    ...know my roots are firmly planted, forever I shall stay

Dream Angel

It is nocturnal insanity…
Electric storms of thought
Remove all gravity from sleep
A passion from the purest of fires
A beautiful woman causing my soul to leap
		…as sleep keeps me awake

Dreams resurrect me into paradise…
Is that your kiss or a softened whisper
Constantly causing my essence to dart
Or is it how when you give me a hug
You also have your hands around my heart
		…The magical place of your embrace

It is chaos of the flesh…
I confess in my desire to touch you
Longing to be imprisoned within your flesh
To get lost within our unchained thoughts
Taste the passion of elated tears and sweat
		…This lonely man burning begins to shake

Can I spend the night in your mind…
Awakening brings a delicate combination
I crave your rapture with all that I am
Left desiring your thoughts be mirrorized
Knowing in fact that you are flesh and blood
Left begging as you arise, you vision myself in your eyes
		…You fill mine nightly with your grace

Jester's Funeral

Six feet of dark earth piled in mass
Oaken casket lowered slowly into the grave
Attending the court jester's funeral
In his velvet slumber is he still playing the fool's slave

For it is when we watch them ascend
The moment another's soul comes to arise
That we read all the terms and conditions
Of our own life's simulated guise and disguise

This man of humor, wit, and juggling skills
Built a pillar of joy for others each day
Never allowing his personal pain to remain
Always putting his talents upon public display

Thinking once that I was mighty
Connecting the dots that truth often hides
He was passed the cup from a modern apprentice
To bring smile's to others dreary lives

Living his life ahead of the storm
Spinning a tale for a loaf of bread
How was I to know the breath of this ghost
Would effect my thinking more now that he is dead

In the end, do we all not
At some point vanish in our sleep
Is there any joy that we have shared
That will cause others to stop and weep

~continued~

Leaning heavily against a headstone pillar
Wondering why we always count value in jewels
Raising a toast to the man who's salary came in smiles
It is the rest of us, not the court jester
Who always play the role of life's fool

A Sword Named Wisdom

Blood soaked memories
Within eyes of blazing hate
The power of omens fractured his soul
Leaving him to this last dying fate

Upon this craggy edge
He stops one final time
Reminiscing of a day he was whole
When Camelot was sublime

What was the die that cast this man
Leading him down a course of ruination
He once sat proudly at a table of round
A leader in an Elysian collaboration

Remembering once he was a gallant lad
With fortune, virtue, and fame
The only name he now remembers
Is the one for this journey's acclaim

Holding hands gently with his beloved
Strolling slowly through a garden of iris in bloom
This was two score or more years ago
Where he came face to face with his doom

From the sky a mammoth dragon appeared
Landing squarely upon their path
Eyes as black as winter's night
Firestorms spewing from his wrath

~continued~

Saturated in dejection
Having no means at hand to defend
Draco snatched up his loving companion
Flying off with her into a stale wind

Hot liquid bubbled within his heart
Faced with a fervent need for revenge
Grabbing a sword he called wisdom
His honor, loyalty and lady love
All were at stake to defend

Remembering the eyes of his predator
Infected with mangled maggots all in heat
Appearing at once ready to combust
Dining from a buffet of rotted meat

Starting his quest through the mystical forest
Anger impulsions igniting through his core
Unchaining the wolves of his passion
Draco shall not be allowed to live in Camelot anymore

This scavenger of sorrow
Had caused him to bite his pain
How could such a treacherous breed
This type of evil survive within his domain

Revelations abound during each dead night
As every day stagnates into the next
The claws of madness begin to take hold
Ardent ire has his compassion now annexed

~continued~

Traveling through thick elven filled woods
Doing battles with mines filled with trolls
He tells all the tale of his stolen love
Killing all with no knowledge to console

Having traveled through the valley of discontent
Staring upon a mountain pixies once named doom
He wonders wearily upon an evil priestess
A jezebel wearing dragon's blood as her perfume

Her lips move in dark demonic manners
Yet she deceives with a siren's song
Claiming to know how he can end his quest
How to undo this unsightly wrong

Telling our knight in hypnotic ways
His journey is veiled by mordant deceit
You were once guilty of only innocence
Now it is only hatred your pores excrete

I will tell you where the dragons reside
She proclaims with a sardonic grin
However when you face what consumes you
Your energy of discontent must come to an end

She tells him to travel westward
Towards the shores of a sea called sin
There you will find your nemesis Draco
Along the way you will meet his friends

~continued~

Bowing down knee deep in fresh spilt blood
Our knight kisses the slain jezebel's ring
The years have brought leather to his heart
It was now time for Draco to feel his sting

Hearing only the concerto of a desperado
Slaying every dragon threading across his path
Even that two headed beast Devin and Cornwall
Could not overcome this lonely hearts wrath

Scabbard empty, sword in hand
Smelling the sea while crawling up one final hill
The vision of Draco feasting upon the shoreline
Upon the flesh of many he gets his daily fill

Sensing now his time has come
For a battle that may end his fate
Draco claims our hero should have been a day sooner
For his lover was on yesterday's entree plate
Stating that he left her alive
To stare at her beauty day and night
Then getting pleasure from her transformation
As she lost the flicker of her loving light

Before you attempt to take my life
Draco claimed to have wisdom to spew
Telling our knight of the forgotten name
Why it was with his lady that day he flew

I wanted to share with you my poison
Allow you to find out the true loneliness of days
To prove the point that what is good can be bad
When their life is placed in utter disarray

~continued~

Charging now with all his might
With a fury Draco had never before seen
Wisdom sliced through the dragon's heart
A killing blow strong, swift and clean

Slouching now above his quest's prey
What his soul had for so long desired
The knight took a moment to remember
All the evil this dragon had sired

Thinking back now on this journey of hate
He thought of all those he had left crucified
Pondering if the evil that had grown within
Would along with Draco just die

Realizing now his unfinished fate
That Draco had put his honor on a quest
Having failed miserably with his actions
He clutched wisdom firmly with both hands
Ending his pain, running wisdom through his chest

Yesterday's Girl

I remember that moment of joining…
For want of her
My heart was ablaze
Soul impassioned from her fiery skin grip
A single instant forever eternalized
Tasting the moist cherry of her voluptuous lips
      …feeling perpetually lost within a kiss

Not realizing the record would end…
Somehow like a vague memory
Maybe a distant illusion or silken dream
When we kissed my heart always raced the moon
Now just a faint line beats slowly in silent screams
      …now I just talk to myself and reminisce

Within your arms I could see beauty in the darkness…
Two lovers of all passions connecting
Blissfully traveling through unmeasured time
Bodies moving together like the core of a lava lamp
Effortless, in unison, physical affection fervently sublime
      …between each flashing of a summer nights fireflies

Now realizing there is no hope in eternity…
These eyes will always remember
Days before the forlorn ending unfurled
Learning to let go is proves quite difficult
I never thought you would be yesterday's girl
      …your goodbye was the day forever died

The Human Battle

Splintered sentences
Discouraging thoughts
Stomach swirling in circles
Vision covered with spots

No black, No white
Simple shallow gray
Hoping that somehow
This will be a much better day

Whirling emotions
Time standing still
Moving forward in life
Someone give me the will

Tears on the pillow
Night sweats on the sheet
Brain aching with misery
Who turned up life's heat

The day of waste has ended
The night passed on through
Dig out of the abyss
Change the channel and the view

Another day shall begin
I shall not be stuck in the mire
One day can be bad
But not all should be dire

Morose

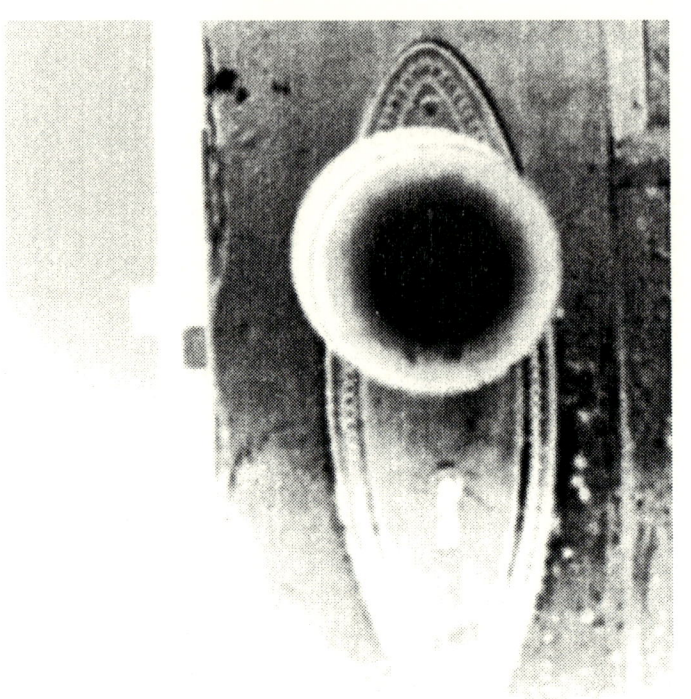

Benighted spirit
Darkness within
Spinning in obscurity
Outlook quite dim
Perpetual stillness
Black is my hue
Shadows surrounding
Bid my smile adieu

~continued~

Souring my happiness
This day has not revealed
A light in my brooding
Sinicism prevails

Gloomy
My essence
All fervor denied
No spiritual movement
No means to provide

I know you are in there
A bright light does reside
Fight through the black hole
In you I confide

Iniquity is no passion
No sinister upside
I rise from the darkness
Opening the door
Reaching for the handle
To my bright soul inside

Just What I Am

Perfection
Not hardly
Flaws and scars galore
Pieces of me have been beaten
Battered to the core

Perfection
Not this man
I have aches
Pains
Tears to shed
Not all pomp
Nor pretty décor
But if you dare
Take a step ahead

Perfection
Not a chance
Many would not give a damn
But if you choose
Step into my world
Know in your heart
I am
Just what I am

Perfection
Not possible
My scars run way too deep
I will proudly show you the outer ones
But the inner exude slowly
Many still cause me to weep

~continued~

Perfection
Not within me
I make mistakes every day
Some cause me embarrassment
Others pain my soul
Causing it to wither away

Perfection
Can be found
If imperfections cause you smiles
Over look them with your exam
Walking into my world
Means you accept me simply because
I am
Just what I am

Blooming Muse

Iris blooms of faith
>That which I have in you
>An impenetrable devotion
>To my heart your name is tattooed

Lily of white emits purity
>As fresh as new felled snow
>Beaten upon by moonlight rays
>Like your smile it radiates a resplendent glow

Orchids represent perfection
>One glimpse of you is validation
>Your aura enlightens the darkest rooms
>Causing all around a tingling sensation

~continued~

Violet symbolizes faithfulness
      My desire to give to you
      My heart, my soul, my everything
      My spirit through and through

Euphorbia is flowing purification
      Like water filtering over the falls
      Your undying love removes impediments
      Permeating perfect ballads from animalist squalls

Yerba Mate grows love and lust
      Two things needed to survive
      Love to keep the flowering blooming
      Lust to allow the blood flow to thrive

Orris guarantees your protection
      Within these arms you shall feel
      No harm can ever come to you
      Allowing past scars to quickly heal

Uva Ursa has psychic powers
      Foretelling all that is true
      Each day I awake, I simply know
      I am more than in love with you

Keeper of My Soul

Hey beautiful…
Of free will and testament
My neural pulses wildly pound
Dreaming of walking hand in hand
Leaving our foot prints upon the sand
    …You leave me vulnerable

Clarity in…
The reflecting lakes
Filling the space of your eyes
Dancing like blue moon gypsies
Fully surrounded by nymphalid butterflies
    …All that glitters in your soul

If I could have one wish…
There is only one place for you
A permanent loving taste and embrace
With loves cylinders erupting like wild fires
Within the constant perfection of your smiling face
    …I would be heaven in your mind

When two become one…
The world becomes glitter
Floating elegantly through ones aura
Causing all pressures to drift quickly away
As we swim in the liquid sugar of each others lips
    …We do not have to dream all alone

~continued~

The best day of my life...
Cupid shot wisely with his bow
Leaving me on a bridge named surrender
Gently tossing my feelings, my worries to the wind
Knowing within your arms I could be manly, yet tender
   ...You tore through my gruff exterior with love

Hey Beautiful...
   ...You are the keeper of my soul

Son of a Gardner

Azure waters filled the sightline
No moon to excite an undertow
You could hear the calming of silence
From this gloriously perched plateau

In search of a personal parable
A mad mission for inner strength
To light the torch with all answers
That will keep a muddy conscious at arm's length

I hear the maddening elegance
From further and further away
You have rung your late evening bell
Sending the paupers like me away

Through days of obligation
Tending to your garden's needs
Ensuring mauve and chartreuse
Are not simply growing purples or greens

There is no need for you to miss me
You have no knowledge I exist
I am simply the lowly gardener
Admiring you through smiling tears of mist

No justice within my cradle
No blood running thick in caste or class
I ponder the ancient sorrow
Invisible to your present, future and past

~continued~

From my seat upon this mountain
My imagination glimpses what should be
Ridiculous thoughts and dreams
That from your balcony you stare at your garden
Thinking passionate romantic thoughts of me
There are days I fill with the notion
That I could simply become the rain
In order for you to see and feel
How this heart is full of pain

Could you look within the cover
Can I cast upon you a spell
Help clarify this confusion
Is not within the heart
Where one's true wealth dwells

Being the son of a poor man
Yes he was a gardener too
He told me tales of a beautiful girl
She turned out to be the woman in you

Why must all in your world be white
Find some shiny shades of gray
One cannot wear more than one pair of shoes
Nor everyday love the way I do today

My seat tonight, really has no view
It all lives within my smitten mind
Yet when the morning sun does rise
Your gardens will cry out to me
Next to your love, they are my prize

~continued~

This night I found my parable
Holding it close as my last embrace
Your diamonds and riches may dazzle others
True beauty lies within the smile upon your face

One lonely heart can be satisfied
Showing his love to be true
By ensuring each morning that you arise
That all of the blooms in your garden
Continue glistening a lustrous beauty like you

Black Silk Stockings

There can be no hiding
Arousal emoting from her eyes
A night on the town his promise
Her repayment, no disguise

Black silk stalking rolls slowly
Over the calf, up the thigh
Sensing his glare from across the room
Seeing a sparkle from his eye

This summer dress intoxicating
Showing every bump
Each luscious curve
Snugly surrounding her body
His treasure this night to observe

Her smile cries out she is hungry
Not for the food for which they wait
Her aura an erotic mood
All dressed up for the evening
For dinner they may be late

Hormones in a brood
Dinner reservations ticking away
Her sweet perfume fills the air
He succumbs to its sweet bouquet

Sauntering over slowly
Turning the lights down soft and low
She gently whispers, "I want you"
He shivers from head to toe
Black silk stocking rolls smoothly
Down her thigh and to the floor
Just the thought of an evening away
Brought arousal, ambient amore

Liberation

My dreams liberated...
Through a natural progression of caring
You have confiscated something of mine
My heart and soul are in your command
For just the kiss of your shadow I pine
              ...our destination undefined

Spellbound and speechless...
Once feeling nameless and faceless
Now one lifetime is not long enough to sip
Feeling the need to eternally savor
To taste all the sweetness from your lips
              ...to your fervid honey I succumb

Within your eyes...
Symmetrically perfect, walking arm in arm
I fight gravity, ascending simply from contact
Staring intensely into your sparkling solitaires
Discharging sensations of elation along my nerve tract
              ...celestial sanctuary I find

Your love is now...
Every sentence I now whisper
Every temptation that comes ablaze
Every bud I now see flowering
Comes from the passion within your gaze
              ...everything I have become

Erasing the Blue

Invisible wounds
Covering acres of skin
Incisions from not loving at all
You rode right in
On a honeyed summer wind
To soften a heart from its fall

Standing before me
On neutral ground
With courtly beauty and grace
You have a way without words
An aura of utopian penache
Causing this slate of loneliness to erase

Without uttering a sound
Your eyes whisper to me
For eternity we shall get lost
On a mountain top, a tropical isle
Maybe within a sea of foam green
Maybe stroll through a bamboo forest
Our personal nirvana, loving and serene

As time strolls us along
With my heart in your palms
Remembering your first touch, sugared smell
Veering me from tsunamic teardrop waves
Aiding me to bid perpetual loneliness farewell

Fading Reflections

Within all visible reflections
In search of all my heart desires
Hearing the sounds, the melodic euphony
From a string less violin, strumming for an all mute choir

Passions quest
An eternity of dreams
Abandoned pools as tear ducts dry
I was not nearly as good at uttering hello
As you were at enunciating goodbye

Wasted love
Labeled upon crimson winds
I was a sweet castaway within your eyes
Never realizing
There is a thorn in every heart
Causing yours to sharpen was my demise

You laughed at my pain
Another blow to my bruise
Sitting here just letting time pass me by
Retention of fading illusions
These eyes must never remember
All of the moments you caused me to cry

The four basic human necessities
Food, water, shelter, and love
May not be required for all we meet
She who loves the flicker of her own flame
Will always be emotionally incomplete

~continued~

Neurons flood through my conundrum
Who was this captor of my soul
Wanting to give no liberation date
Now is time to make my own parole

Thoughts of your hold come full circle
My very breath a personal serenade
Time to embrace every ray of sunshine
As your reflection slowly fades away

One Bite

The setting sun bleeding crimson red
A fitting sight for a heart altered to blue
Trying to hike away the abscesses of love
Remove the sting of words that shot through

Stumbling upon a rope bridge crossing
One to which I had been blind during strolls past
Leading me to an unhinged, rusted cemetery gate
In the middle was a pit of embers and floating ash

Marching through a garden of blooming dandelions
Kicking their seed about to spread them anew
Lying next to the fire pit that had lost its breath
Was a diary entitled "Carnivorous Desires are not Taboo"

The setting sun passed to a shimmering moonlight
No flashlight needed in order to peruse
Reading maddening tales that curse the sunrise
Also, the intense power one trickle of blood can infuse

No longer pondering my own lovelorn miseries
The throes of my own rejection's meanings now lost
Intricately woven words of a lost soul's pangs
The immense desecration one taste of eternity can exhaust

She had embraced the emptiness of that darkest night
Taken captive by the sweet sickness of her lover's thirst
Not understanding the finality of his sleek words of desire
Just feeling the dams of her womanhood preparing to burst

~continued~

Sitting here alone in the mid of night
The final chapter of her tale brought things clear
Having felt that she was bitterly betrayed by the vamp
Some parts of her soul she would forever hold dear

She would never take a sip of the crimson heat
The essence that will allow her body to thrive
Without first knowing her next lover understood his fate
Sharing only each other's thick liquid to eternally revive

Once thinking all of my own tear ducts had dried
That only my own soul bared stitches and scars
A river poured down my cheeks this night
Wondering if this woman's bones lie bare under the stars

Hearing movement from behind the largest stone
Turning quickly, I let out a thin piercing shriek
Marching towards me veiled in a fog of loneliness
She said, "for a decade I have been waiting for you"
As sandpaper skinned hands wiped the tears from my cheek

Unable to partake in the wine of her essence
Her rough appearance sped up by the weavers of time
Yet even with only moonlight beaming down
One could tell she was a beauty during her prime

With eyes an odd arrangement of color
One pitch black, the other light blue
She had hair as course as a desert of sand
Held to a wrinkled scalp by rain drops and glue

~continued~

Sitting back down alarmed with trepidation
She offered her hand as a gesture to calm my fear
Feeling the beauty of her soul beyond pale skin
So much more than the handfuls of nothing
Most lovers try to find a manner in which to endear

Orating the meaning behind the words upon her page
Telling her story a manner to channel her everlasting pain
With a voice that could bring the butterflies to dance
Sedating my mind as she sung praises to sacred love's domain

Remembering the emptiness of love's near and far
Fearless I stood to give her my warm embrace
Telling her for the feeling of a love sung so pure
She could drink from my veins that were beginning to race

Feeling the erase of all my poisons past
Yearning as I place my moist lips upon her face
Finding joy in the jagged coral of her cracked lips
Anticipating the moment of this vamps first taste

Placing her jagged teeth upon my bare neck
Like a slow drug she teased before the plunge
Then the fire began dancing through my veins
Squeezing thick velvet from my neck like a sponge

Lying under bright stars happy and bleeding
No one could be prepared for this latest surprise
The ash of her pale skin now converted to pink
You could see azure oceans within both of her eyes

~continued~

Pulling me into her bosom so fair
Assuring me her heart is true to her verse
Letting me know that the eternal night is ours to share
Bonded by our souls as well as our curse for thirst

What irony of finding a love to never be lost
Hiking about to pour whisky upon sour wounds
Finding someone with which
To share life by each other's drops
Tasting with passion of each others flesh
Under each and every moon

Poems, Prayers, and Promises

Poems, prayers, and promises
Simple gifts I give to you
No monetary value
Just words that are my glue

The poems share my feelings
My inner soul
My wit
My doubt
Letting you look upon me
Get to know me
My feelings for you
Inside and out

My prayers for you are simple
Happiness
Joy
Delight
May God look down upon you
Guide you with his bright light

These promises are simple
To you I will always be
One shoulder to cry upon
A voice of reason
When in need
Lover
Friend
Companion
During dark days
Marching through light
My poems, prayers and promises
Are simply all this man can guarantee
Each and every night

The Quest for Excalibur

In the monastery garden
Where the dragons once playfully danced
Hearing the call of a maiden's prayer
One must crusade to take the chance

Go to where the rainbows chant
You will hear the wind's lament
Walk towards the turquoise flame
Your Excalibur awaits in dried cement

The conversation left me reluctant
Yet the moment our eyes converged
The shape of her face left me crying
In a hug our bodies slowly merged

Her tear drops glistened pure desire
The eyes a reflecting pond
She asked me to leave,
To be the guardian of her flame
From this day forward, and beyond

On a quest to chase down this artifact
Hoping to attract the maiden's prosperity
Followed by countless black butterflies
Songs without words my verity

Keep stepping forward I chant to myself
Each stride carrying the tune of a broken harp
No one bellowing farewell to a returning hero
As I view the dalliance of eagles upon a nearing scarp

~continued~

Can I be this miracle worker
Causing dancing at the maiden's gate
Will sorrow be the only one to call
If Excalibur causes me to wait

Trekking through changes of season
Now chilled from enchanting winds
Is there really an end to a rainbow
Will I caress my fair maiden again

Embracement of possibilities
Fire spirits catching strength from my heart
Can I find a personal synchronicity
On a quest set to doom from the start

Reading her unwritten letter
I have grown accustomed to her face
It is as lovely as the blooming rose
I must find this sword swiftly,
Or for my tears find a resting place

Toward the one
Through molten rain
Through valleys with names like despair
A hint of shimmer, a glimmer of hope
The final kiss of a rose I still wear

Spring breaks upon a waterfall
Glistening colors sing bright and strong
I walk through, sitting upon a rock
Is a knight I learned of through song

~continued~

My tale is one that astounds him
He smiles as he explains my true quest
Excalibur resides within you
Your maiden has put you to a test

What of the sword, I proclaim with fervor
He said you carry one in your hand
But to defend your maiden, to slay her dragons
My friend, your own heart and mind you must command

Having learned that the distance is short
From mouth to heart and back
I carry my sword, Excalibur
To defend my maiden from attack

The Path of the Mistress

She cares not about the way I dress...
Life shows us so many paths to follow
Some straight and narrow and others curved
It is in the fall when my mistress takes my hand
I realize any and all paths have beauty to be observed
    ...or that I am not a drop dead handsome man

~continued~

Her embrace always leaves me enchanted...
Upon an apparent endless journey she leads me
Over various lush grasses and broken stones
Into my ear she whispers "location is everything"
As she marches off into some great unknown
    ...a lustrous beauty beaming as far as the eye can scan

She is always only one breath away...
Our walks in autumn have become my annual favorite
She shares her oaks of russet and hickories of golden bronze
Her sugar maples are ablaze with a brilliant orange red
The red maples have a bright scarlet coat tried on
    ...no matter if we are minutes or miles apart

My mistress and I have a divine history...
The chilling wind bites as the moon touches my shoulder
Awakening me to the fact my Lady of Autumn shall soon take on ice
Sealing this beautiful season with the most cutting of winter kisses
Dreams of a spring stroll amongst blistering blooms
To survive the winter this shall have to suffice
    ...Mother Earth has captured a portion of my heart

Your Lips

Oh I remember
Your lips so divine
Pressing firmly
Touching softly
Up against mine

Oh I remember
Your lips so divine
Sweeter and richer
Than the first press of the vine

Lips so divine
I could never forget
The tenderness
The feeling
Luscious and wet

Oh I remember
I remember
I will never forget

Burning

A sensuous tingle
Trickles slowly
Up my spine
Your long nails
Running
Into my skin
I am at your command
Heart, soul, and mind
Supine

You kiss me
Just once
Was all that was required
The soft gentle touch
Envelops my desires
My urges
Fully awake
Passions
On fire

Shaking
Trembles
Quivers
Hot chills
That one simple touch
Your lips
That kiss
The thrills

~continued~

Shuddering
At the thought
Of what may lie ahead
What rage
What passion
Ripped clothing
To a shred
A simple touch
A kiss
A batting of eyes
Simple things
Still causing
My arousal
This sea of fire
To arise

Compos Mentis

Lucid dreaming
A moment of peace
We know the night
Let me breath in your release

We are alone with everybody
All harm ends here
You are buoyancy
Renovation
These dreams of you persevere

I see the sway of your torso
Run fingers along the small of your back
You are an elusive lady
Yet each night these dreams attack

Many mornings
Many moods
Changing priorities from day to day
Yet each night is filled
With your enchantress fanfare
I sleep in your perfume
It's sweet bouquet

Enter slumber's gravity
The pillow cuts with content
Every little kiss
A pleasurable torment

~continued~

A good ending
To every bad day
Your dream sketches
Keep me alive
You are my soul's kleptomaniac
On your nightly renovations
Our joining
This man recharges and revives

Firsts

Something tenderly refreshing...
Moments of ethereal shared passions
Man's last emotion sparkles within his eyes
A brief glimpse through his pupils into the soul
The blazing currents testify you are his prize
        ...that may never be washed away

Affectionate by nature...
Nerves leave oration operations unstable
Perspiration glistens upon all exposed skin
The moment of bold truth fumbles into timidity
Love can leave even a lothario blushing chagrin
        ...inducing thoughts to process in disarray

Delicate flows to sentimental...
Hearts dance understanding the consequence
Veins throbbing so hard they may burst
He is not afraid to love you completely
Allow the velvet realm of your lips quench his thirst
        ...Leaving mentation stirring awhirl

Get the moment right man...
Nothing can be held more sacred
Not even the erotic pressing together of flesh
Than the first moment pairs of uncertain quivering lips
Unite as one in a gentle, resplendent interlocking mesh
        ...reach out and kiss the girl

Elemental

Earth...
An avalanche of somatic sensations
Tremors and earthquakes rumble within
Just dreaming of the scent of your hair
Or the soft tender touch of your skin

Fire...
Just seeing the sparkle within your eye
Understanding the angelic soul from which it came
Sensing we are moving to an immortal sunburst finish
You furnish the oxygen to feed my inner flame

Air...
The gentle whisper of a northerly wind
Can leave subtle impressions upon one's skin
Goosebumps, shivers, and tingles of joy
Much as the thoughts of holding you
Once forever
Then again and again

Water...
Your spirit flows euphorically through me
A rainbow spectrum cascading over a fall
Moony thoughts of tasting your luscious lips
Bring roaring rapids and passionate squalls

Spirit...
Reaching out you grabbed my soul
Giving me love, then self-esteem
Always keep your eyes upon the sky
You attached wings upon my dreams

A Sorceress Rides Through

Mumbling to myself incoherently
Alone in the cold of the rain
Ponder afterlife's existence
Am I going places or into the pain

Is all I possess at this very moment
My own little heaven, all I deserve
Or should memories of future actions
Be something worthy to preserve

Slumping here in the deepest of thought
Shivering, with a hammer firmly in my hand
Am I just a thief upon a cross
Is there more to this life and beyond,
One truly must understand

Thunder clamors in the distance
A sorceress rides through
I give her my surrender
I had nothing else to do

She asked me why life's struggles
Put me in a sensitive mood
I explained we all have boats to build
Hoping all of our sins have not accrued

She shrieked a lonesome whistle
Then spoke loudly with two tongues
Her eyes were candlelit scars
From her breath radium rain duly sprung

~continued~

She asked how much time was left
What alibi's I would give
To be a part of the soul serenade
Where forever one may live

I explained that when my casket shifts
At the time the water becomes wide
He promised to remember all the good things I have done
Knowing my love is much stronger than my pride

This sorceress became frustrated
Threatening me with violent dreams
There are now cowboys with cell phones I said
The world must soon be ending, or so it seems

Life is full of lovers, liars, and losers
Leaving me worn and broken
But one's faith can always rule the day
Even if sometimes, it is left unspoken

I removed the dust from my bible
As the sorceress flew away
I swayed myself to a long remembered melody
About an unbroken circle,
As for the first time in years
I knelt down to pray

Daddy's Healing Rain

Sweeter than sea breezes
Vivacious with your smile
You continue to steal my heart
From the day you were born
Life has seemed so much more worthwhile

Time to reflect
More than two years have passed by
You are lollipops and roses
Happiness
An apple in the eye

Language barriers breaking
You know so much more
Each and every passing day
You amaze me to smiles and tears
With the silly, yet brilliant things you say

You are innocence and power
All tied up into one
Noise is your ritual
No singing left undone

Everything that touches you
Becomes a passion to the end
You engulf every flowers essence
Every crayon color you blend

~continued~

We now sing together
Not just daddy crooning you
Growing independence
Everything is "my turn"
All avenues you pursue

The sadness in growing to fast
Makes happiness all the same
All these little magic moments
Of all these things you are
You are daddy's daily healing rain

Love's Echo

THE ONE...

Did you feel...
When all around has fallen
When my life's flame wrenches blue
I just simply have to say your name
To bid melancholic thoughts adieu
... the mountains tremble

Could you sense...
You are a sundrop within the rainshine
Scarlet flowers within a chartreuse range
Anywhere with you in this world becomes paradise
Bringing conclusion to the adage
All who are lovers must be deranged
... the wind's sad songs depart

Are you listening...
Each and every time I look at you
I find myself wishing for a clean pure pair of eyes
Knowing now what dreams look like
Within the orbs of your sweet spring skies
... for thumping whispers within

They are love's echoes...
Your lips form a passionate kiss of the future
Waiting to taste them I forget how to breathe
Your soul performs for me virtuoso
Please never cure me of cupid's disease
... from every chamber of my heart

...WORTH DYING FOR

Blasphemy

If time truly loves a hero...
The modern lothario has the role of player
Today's maidens are tired of his contemptuous games
Awaiting the arrival of their dashing paladins
Who will treat them with dignity while lighting their flames
    ...for actions courageous, true and just

Do the ladies love the great romantic...
Feeding her passions with a gentle kiss
Holding her twice to make her feel secure
Loving her tears with a shoulder strong yet soft
Allowing her to flirt in manners coy and demure
    ...for sharing sweetened passions instead of raw lust

Ancient words long ago written...
Times may never change ideals of valor and grace
The beastly lothario is not just a current fiend
Knights and paladins shall always conquer the day
When it is time for love and romance to convene
    ...a gallant way of life once contrived

"Blasphemy" is today's modern knight's battle cry...
The paladin's soul stays wet from tears of joy
As his maiden happily mends to his battle wounds
Plush reflections of her beauty sparkles within his eyes
As a vast chorus of mysterious ballads from hidden harps
Forever keeps their heartbeats synchronically attuned
    ...it is our declaration that chivalry shall survive

The Taming

Jackie was frustrated as she turned the key in her convertible Lexus. How on earth could she have agreed to go visit John at his new house? She had seen his living quarters many times before. John and his ex-college fraternity brothers, with their keg filled brothel of madness and no ability to clean.

Jackie, only John was allowed to call her by that name. In the six years since college she had evolved into Jaqueleen, the power hungry businesswoman who had her eyes on the dollars and no zest for anything that did not evolve around work. Jaqueleen did not care that everyone in the office called her "a bitch on wheels" behind her back, or that they mumbled the only way she could have gotten so high up in the company was to sleep with any number of 70 year old partners. She had arrived and she always brought with her an attitude, she thought she smelled of success. Yet everyone in the office knew she would never be happy because no man in the world would put up with her shit for the length of time it would take to get her clothes off.

She started seeing John her junior year of college and still had a sweet spot for him despite ALL of his shortcomings. He did not care about money or wealth, he showed no desire for power or control of anything, and John decided to live his life day by day. He went to college, got his degree, and then decided to go work for his dad in order to take over the family butcher shop. That is no way to apply an MBA Jackie always mumbled to herself in his presence. She saw John as a little kid with a beer bong and a set of golf clubs. Yet, there was something in his eyes that always melted her even when she hated him and his lack of desire the most.

~continued~

So what could this meeting be all about? John had been pestering her for five months now to come see his new place when they would meet for a quick lunch or a late night dinner and drink. This on again off again romance always ended with Jaqueleen taking control and reminding John that he needed to grow up and get a real job. She would often say this at a baseball game with John and his crew of clowns having hot dog eating contests or squirting mustard from the little packets on other patrons in the lower section.

As the wind blew through her strawberry-blonde hair and the sun was hitting her just right, she looked ravishing tonight she admitted as she stared in the rearview mirror. Wearing a $700 pants suit that she used as a power statement in today's board meeting, she wondered why she was wasting this day of personal perfection on John, silly boy John this evening. She should be out wining and dining some politician or businessman with clout so she could make further advances in the business world.

Looking at the directions she downloaded from the Internet, Jackie new she was close to her destination. As she pulled into the driveway she was in total shock. She had expected to see a yard in need of mowing, beer cans all over the lawn and some form of women's undergarments hanging from the ceiling fan on the porch. Much to her dismay, there were perfectly manicured gardens of hydrangeas, rose bushes, and even one garden of wildflowers with sunflowers growing proudly to form a back edge. The grass was plush, the darkest of greens which was rare for the late august sun.

As Jackie stepped onto the screened in front porch she noticed the furniture was immaculate, the house freshly painted, and she smelled a cinnamon candle burning in the corner. Upon a table was a single red rose in a vase. Leaning against it was a card with her name neatly printed on the envelope. Overwhelmed by the entire scene, she opened

~continued~

the envelope, taking in the sweet scent of the rose as she read. Jackie, it said, please let yourself in to my humble abode when you arrive. I am in the kitchen cooking one of your favorite meals. There is a bottle of sparkling wine opened and awaiting you to free the bubbles from the confines of the bottle, which contains its sweetness.

Opening the door cautiously, still expecting to see four months worth of dirty underwear piled in a corner and enough dust on top of the tables that you can write your name freehand, she was again left in shock. Everything was clean, as if a maid service had lived here for a week. Even the tops of the perfectly matched artworks upon the walls were dust free. Then the smell of garlic hit her and forced her to smile. John was making shrimp scampi just for her. But wait, this cannot be the same man she had known for all these years. John was the one who always told the joke that men knew it was time to change their boxers if they flung them at the wall and they stuck, but they had a day or two left it they did not cling to the paint. Where, she thought to herself, did he learn how to cook as well?

Hearing her talking to herself, John walked into the room. He was dressed in an exquisite pin striped suit, shirt pressed and starched, hell even his socks matched, which was a major accomplishment for John. Jaqueleen had now officially left the room and Jackie arrived. For the first time in her life she was speechless. John motioned for her to come sit at the table, poured her a glass of the bubbly and went back into the kitchen. Returning with the first course, a beautiful garden salad with ruby red ripe cherry tomatoes, shaved carrot, and the greenest lettuce leaves she had ever seen. John, bragging for a brief moment stated that when they were done eating he would show her his vegetable garden in the back yard where all aspects of this dish had been grown. Jackie let out a large sigh, looked John in the eye and said, "Just when the hell did you learn how to cook, grow plants and vegetables, and iron your own fucking shirts John?"

~continued~

John smiled a big shit-eating grin and said, "Jackie darlin, I have always known how do to these things, you just never bothered to ask."

As the evening went on, John had started playing some Marvin Gaye and The Reverend Al Green as background music. They talked, she bragged on how she had lowered the boom on the testicles in the board meeting today, and John spoke of how his father had decided to retire due to a bad back. This left John in charge of the meat market, and in the three months since his father's retirement, John had expanded the store and added two other stores in different parts of town. Just hearing those words made Jackie ponder if she had read him all wrong over the years due to his friends, or if he had some form of epiphany that changed his perspective. She was not going to press the issue because her pager had just gone off and she had to excuse herself to make an "incredibly important" call. Business was after all what made her the total package she was today, even though she knew herself she was a reclusive bitch in the office.

Upon her return into the living room, Jackie noticed John had dimmed the lights, turned off the music and lit several candles for ambiance. He yelled from the other room for her to please take a seat on the couch and he would be with her shortly.

John walked in carrying an acoustic guitar. Jackie again did not know that John had any musical talents beyond being able to belch several verses of Stairway to Heaven after hitting a beer bong.

Bending down to one knee, holding the guitar on the other, John stared her squarely in the eyes. He starts by saying he has dreamt of this moment for years, but never had the courage to do so. John added that yes, he had made a number of life changes, altered his friends, taken responsibility for the business and learned many new things. All in the hopes he stated that he would win the heart of the one true love of his

~continued~

life. He stared Jackie deep in the eyes; she could see the fire burning within his soul through his crystal clear blues.

Jackie began to tremble all over her body, her palms were sweaty with anticipation, her thoughts running wild, when John began playing the guitar and sang from his heart a song he had written for her entitled "Have You Ever." It was when he strummed for the first note she saw the diamond glowing upon his pinky.

I still vividly remember
The sharp teeth of that winter wind
Its numbing effects lifting my burdens
I closed my eyes ever so slowly
Then you kissed me for the first time, again

My senses overwhelmed that very first night
You told me you loved only me true
I shall hold forever the scent of violet delight
And the touch of velvet skin with a pink hue

Have you ever fallen in love
That first moment when moist lips turn dry
Finding salvation within the arms of another
Animal magnetism in monumental supply

Have you ever felt the passion
The relentless need to never cease to dream
Where someone's sunny smile
Transforms all that is gray to pinks and greens

Knowing this is the beginning of my finest hour
Learning more than ordinary miracles can happen for me
This beautiful fool shall drink sacrifice from his cup
Please do not make me wait as I am on bended knee

~continued~

Have you ever fallen in love
That first moment when moist lips turn dry
Finding salvation within the arms of another
Animal magnetism in monumental supply

Have you ever felt the passion
Felt the sting of amore's loving embrace
Waltz with me through this masquerade ball of life
Allow the meaning of this ring to forever
Be a symbol of the smile you put upon my face

I shall always vividly remember
The feeling of your lips pressed firmly to mine
As we tuck each other into bed each night
Feeling a true love beyond the divine

Just as John struck his final note, Jackie had tears flowing from her eyes. Then the unthinkable happened. Her boss was calling her on her cell phone. She stared at the phone lighting up, but had to think, what to do at this crucial moment. Jumping up she answered the phone, John could hear her boss yelling that she needed to be back downtown ASAP to help close a deal that was huge for the company. Jackie soon transformed into her role of Jaqueleen and responded that she would be there shortly and show those little morons exactly who was in charge and get this deal done.

John stood there stunned as she hung up. She stared at him and saw the pain in his eyes. This had been his moment, his crowing achievement in their relationship, and now after all he had done, he was still only second fiddle for the bitch on wheels. She said she was sorry, but that she had to go and rushed out of his house. As she reached the highway, the tears started flowing from her eyes. Had she done the right thing? Would he ever forgive her? Could she ever face him again

~continued~

after basically slamming his balls into a vice and squeezing until they burst? She decided that the only thing that was important now was to close this deal, it was real life, it was what made her tick, romance could wait until she was 45, wealthy beyond all measures, and needed a boy toy to keep her happy.

Jaqueleen made it to the office in time to salvage the deal for her boss. But at what cost for her chances of a life with someone who loved her? She sat alone at her desk until four a.m., pondering, remembering, just thinking of those moments over the past eight or so years that John had made her smile. She reminisced about that first night they made love. Yes, it was a cold winter night as she recalled. Of course his song did not include the part about the policeman showing up and shining his light into her face as she was riding him in the backseat of his car. She must move on she finally concluded. She must face the fire and reach her goals of power, esteem, civic acknowledgement and business savvy. She must be the "bitch on wheels" until she had amassed all of this and more. She was driven. John would just get in the way of her dreams. Having him come home smelling like raw beef and vegetables every night while she was attempting to wine and dine a client was unacceptable. He was expendable, she would never call him again or answer his calls. Yet when she made that decision, she felt her heart ache. She then just told herself it was indigestion from all the garlic in the scampi and put him in the wastebasket of her mind.

John spent the next three nights staring at the ceiling. He knew deep down in his heart that he had made the right choice. He knew that in spite of all Jackie's power trips, her dreams of grandeur, and her wants of power, that she was the one for him. His trip down this road began about eight months before when he read some Shakespeare. Yes, William Shakespeare and not the cliff note's versions always used in college to get a passing grade and still have beer drinking time. He was taken in by the tale "The Taming of the Shrew." Although Jackie was

~continued~

not a "Shrew" in the purest sense of the word, he understood his calling concerning her and his life. He knew deep down she had goodness in her heart, she had love within her soul and passion all throughout her every essence. It was when he had finished reading it the third time he knew he had changes to make. He had been trying to get her over to his new abode for many months to show her how he had altered his lifestyle. Just telling her would not suffice, she must see the evidence. Now his work had taken an interesting turn, should he continue on? YES he screamed out the window, she is worth every ounce of energy. John knew he was a handsome man to many women, but in the end, his heart held only one true love. Jackie, not Jaqueleen, oh how he loathed to hear her repeat that name to her employees to make sure they pronounced it correctly. He would not fail, he had made huge strides in maturing, had taken ownership of his own life and now knew, no, he saw it as a predestined fate that he tames the beast Jaqueleen.

It had been more than two weeks since Jackie had run out on John when his first attempt at contact was made. She arrived at the office late on a Monday morning to find a bouquet of red roses and white tulips sitting upon her desk. There must have been two-dozen of each in this masterpiece of a setting that covered two-thirds of her desk. The card simply read "I love you Jackie, have a marvelous day" Signed John. She thought about this for about three seconds then her phone rang and it was the boss, she had to run to his office for an emergency meeting of the minds. As she passed all the employees in the cubes, they all looked at her funny. She felt their odd stares and knew they must be thinking one of the partners or some slimy client she slept with sent her that monstrosity of a flower fest. She immediately used her cell to call her secretary and have it removed to the lobby for décor.

As Wednesday rolled around she came back from a meeting to find a to go order of scampi from her favorite Italian restaurant in town sitting on her desk. Delivered by the owner himself with a salad and

~continued~

154

fresh bread. Martino, the owner, said that he had missed her and John coming to his place together and sharing in his bountiful plates of food. He had called John and he stated that you were far to busy anymore to make it out and that I should deliver this to you each Wednesday so you never forget the good times had within the candles of my place. He then set down a little music box and pushed play as he walked out. "Fly Me To The Moon" by Frank Sinatra started playing softly. Jackie stopped for a moment, then caught herself. She told herself it would not be that easy for her, she must push on being the eternal bitch and reach her goals.

Friday's had become a special delivery day as well. Each Friday morning a box of her favorite chocolate truffles would arrive from the Godiva shop down the road. In the afternoons, when she usually took a few moments to unwind from the week a large box of chocolate covered strawberries and a thermos of cocoa would be delivered by some unknown delivery boy. Week after week this happened, Monday's with flowers, Wednesday with scampi and Friday's with chocolate. It had now been three months and John had yet attempt to call, but had made his presence felt. The pressure of her job was wearing her thin at the moment and at times she was thankful for his thoughts and gifts. It was the following week that would do her heart in, she would finally break.

That next Monday her flowers arrived with the usually have a great week card from John, but this time there was something else. With it came a cassette recording of John singing his song of love to her, the same one he had serenaded her with upon bended knee with a ring on his finger to give her. On Wednesday, Martino brought his food again, but this time the music was not Frank, no, it was John again singing the same ballad proclaiming his love for Jackie. On Friday, her boss started her day getting her riled up about one simple mistake she had made that cost them a deal. It was her first mistake in over six years of

~continued~

155

service, but he would not let it end. When she returned to her office the chocolates made her smile and she herself pushed play on the recorder. It was at the moment she knew. True happiness was not about money, it was not about fame, and it was not even about stature. It was simply about following one's heart, and John had done so in not giving up on her.

She rushed from her office, screaming at her secretary she was leaving for the day. Her assistant was stunned because that bitch never left early on a Friday so she herself could do the same. She drove all the way to John's house with a smile on her face as she played his cassette in her car. She felt the love in his voice and wondered why in the hell she had been such a fool to ignore the call of the wild, the need of her inner beast, to just unleash her passion and let go. It was five p.m. when she pulled into his driveway and she noticed his vehicle was in the garage. As she approached the door she saw a note with her name taped on the handle. She opened the note which simply stated "it took you long enough, now get in here!"

Jackie had planned this moment out to the best of her ability. Yes she still wanted to be in charge, but not totally and not as one would think. John walked up to her and she asked him "How in the hell did you know I would be coming out here today?" John responded truthfully, "I did not know it would be today, or tomorrow, or next week. I have had that note up there since the first week you were gone, just waiting for you to come to your senses and realize how perfect we are for one another." Jackie rushed into John's arms and gave him the warmest, deepest kiss she had ever given another in her life. She felt the warmth of his arms, their hearts were beating in tune and her eyes were now flowing like a wild mountain waterfall. She then sat John on the couch, the very same couch she had sat many months before, and got down on her knees. She said to John, "I have put you through so much, but you have made me realize a few things. I can never stop

~continued~

hearing your beautiful ballad to me within my thoughts. I do not have a gorgeous song for you this night John, but I did write something and hope you will accept my apology for my heinous acts in the past." Jackie had written a poem within her head while sitting at the desk thinking of leaving early, then within the car on her drive.

When it comes to you my love
I have always said the worst thing first
Always thinking that a feast of blood
Would be all I really needed to quench my thirst

Forever dreaming of a house full of riches
Yet to gain them I have been stigmatized
Biting at the hand that was feeding me
Making a name for myself with biting lies

Going through this life all alone
Even if donning a crown and gallant jewels
Cannot bring with it any moments of redemption
Once you have lost your heart and soul who is the fool

I knew one day I would see you again
See the patterns of stars within your eyes
Hopefully fulfilling the prophecy
Tthat we all can find happiness
That true love is a message that everyone should prize

This very moment I shall throw down my sword
Here on my knees, swallowing what is left of my pride
Now visioning the clearing of the path you have laid
I beg you kind sir to allow me to be your humbled bride

~continued~

As Jackie finished reciting her words to John, her cell phone rang and at the same time her pager beeped loudly. Not even bothering to look to see who had called on either, she marched to the door, opened it slowly for effect, and flung both electronic devices as far into the street as she could. They crashed, tumbled and were immediately run over by cars as John and Jackie both laughed heartily.

Jackie knew at this moment Jaqueleen could no longer survive, she needed this man, she needed love, she needed to live life to its fullest. She knew there was no possible way to achieve these goals without this beautiful man by her side. For all the gold in China can be damned and all the jewels one could buy, Jackie felt complete at this moment, with true love standing at her side.

Now Is Mine

Past assemblage of lamentation
Should not be your awakening today
Let Technicolor be your pleasure
May vivid be the color you portray

Allure the image in the mirror
Away from good morning duplicity
Today is a chocolate mood
Take in its taste and simplicity

Wash your brain of its negative syndrome
Quickly remove the ice water from your veins
Pump them full of adrenaline
Every today is beautiful, it is elementary you ascertain

Quit pondering the mystery of being
Know today is NOT the beginning of a similar end
A swing and a miss is only strike one
You get two more chances to ascend

No day is a cookie cutter
The shape of today's dough you yourself define
Everyone is shouting, rooting for you
So come on, repeat after me, "NOW IS MINE"

Lightning Strike

As the phoenix danced...
Life once a faded tapestry
No equilibrium in my voice to hear
I was a butterfly trapped in a jar of sand
Moonlit shadows reveal the aqueducts of past tears
                    ...around the moon

Reprieve arrived as an...
Digging deep within to find the words
This newfound joy cannot go unexplained
An emotional allegiance to lifetime enjoyment
With you an everlasting place can now easily be obtained
                    ...endless eclipse of the soul

Releasing a felicitous breathe...
During those brief flashing instances
Lightning allows darkness a moment of parole
I will stand bravely upon metal to thank you
For turning this older body into a younger soul
                    ...into eternities scintillating eyes

Amnesty receive for this caged heart ...
Bliss has come from my daily injection
You are my narcotic pure and clean
A smile aglow that burns away dislocated days
Like a postcard received from the most resplendent of dreams
                    ...my spirit rapturously consoled

Status Quo

Hands of chaos mold the world's clay
Fervent winds shriek in tempestuous return
Misery howls of bitterness and sorrow
Masses sit idly getting high upon the flames
Fiddling like Nero as our world burns

Tranquil as statues within our own gardens
Silence nourishes embryotic news network lies
Passively hiding behind brick walls and storm windows
Ignoring the contagiousness of indigent roaring cries

Where now roams the righteous vigilante
Who takes control whenever kindness fails
Are they all scratching at the lids of oaken coffins
Or were all Robin Hoods just alive in fairy tales

Can we afford to wait for another Mother Teresa
To demonstrate what it takes to become a beacon of light
Shall we all just lie dormant in our own happy place
Prophesizing that the millions of the world's hungry
Are being fed by a shining white knight

Is there a prophet somewhere on retainer
Far away in another corner of the world
That will clean the toxic waste from our rivers of sludge
As we lie in front of our Hi-Def televisions
Sipping Coca-Cola in a comfortable fetal curl

~continued~

Have we just come to the realization
That differing religions have and will always be at war
Shall we start taxing those with failed suicide attempts
Just making money from one more person we abhor

It is now time for a dramatic entrance
For the majority to chant out their dreams
So we may all walk barefoot in freedom on Sunday's
Singing forgotten songs of unity and elation
Instead of hearing from our ministers how the world screams

If we were all to aver we are no longer waiting
Would a leader emerge to lead us somewhere
Or do we all just accept the current status quo
Accepting the problems of the world have never changed
That sometimes life is just a long line of unfair

Ego Check

Yesterday within a reflection I found myself...
Not finding an abeyance to the speed of life
Days often spent sprinting just to catch a cold
Chesty ego in a constant hunt of meat for his beast
An inevitable identity crisis gradually unfolds
    ...this run from reality had left me frail

Somehow I thought the fingerless...
Primitively screaming out to act my rage
Involuntary movements creating dark stains
Thinking somehow I had lost my place in line
Rationalizing life's slow easy grind could not entertain
    ...could read a suicide note in Braille

This is my confession...
Appreciative these emotions were yesterday
A smile's brief glimpse never proved me wrong
Infinite combinations of happiness live on for tomorrow
Life is truly best when you are just along for the ride and a song
    ...stupidity had left my ignorance disguised

Often times it is the quiet man...
It is within the journey of one's spirit
To which the truest jubilations are bound
Boldly living this life without any regrets
Brings significance to never turning around
    ...that realizes the beauty in simplicity is prized

Evolution

See me through
I am not finished yet
Person evolving
Through hard work and sweat

Each day I awake
I develop ideals
Working to improve
Mind full of spinning wheels

Whether physical presence
Kindness to share
Sharpening the intellect
Each day in myself
Improvement I do dare

Some days I falter
I take a step back
Making me mortal
Start all over again
Get back on track

Evolution of the human
From melancholy to elation
Each day presents new challenges
Forming a new creation

See me through please
I am still trying to become complete
A human working it out
Through daily work and devotion
Tying to be someone special
You would be proud to meet

The Unfeeling Kiss

The instant it happens
The heart falls sharply down
Eyes shed small tears
Face turns to a frown
You both know it is over
There is something amiss
That dreadful feared moment
The unfeeling kiss

No spark on impact
Dry lips
No emotion
Just pressing together
For public show
Going through motions

The tingle is gone
No quiver
Nor chill
Taste of the lips
It is now bitter
No thrills

Two stepping back
No longer forming one
The kiss tells it all
Heat is undone
A brush of the lips
Once filled with bliss
Surrender is gone
With the unfeeling kiss

Harmonic Angels

A concert of angels
Sing a breathless melody
Calming the wolves of loneliness
Necessity of love this tunes decree

Not a complicated melody
Heart's fallen embers the bouquet
The sheer weight of memories
Lifted and swept away

Harmonic anticipation
Feeling a sense of place
Cradled by their warmth
Echoes of beauty to embrace

Moonlight becomes me
As they serenade a lonely heart
Promising loves reverberations
This heart need not depart

On the way to tomorrow
Out of confusion
A different space
A concert of angels
Sang of future love
Painful memories erased

She Is Beautiful

It was high upon a mountaintop
Standing proudly straddling the continental divide
Mother sun was straight above me at high noon
My shadow flowed gracefully down both sides

In this place time appeared imaginary
Feeling the presence of the guardians of mankind
Embracing this beautiful haven without walls
Freeing all questions without answers from my mind

Sitting down squarely upon the middle
Where water flows forever east or west
Taking in a few moments of silence
Counting the reasons for which I am blessed

Upon this mountaintop I was not alone
There were many here to enjoy this view of life from above
Some appeared to make personal amends with their maker
Others were honeymooners aglow in the flavor of true love

Swept up in this Shangri-la with boundless room to breathe
Where no busy signals eroded the patience of man
No cell phone service, nor answering machines
Sans any biohazard signs for the eyes to scan

Engrossed in the beauty as I rubbed calloused hands
A voice from deep inside my soul would not be denied
Standing unembarrassed I recited the Pledge of Allegiance
Shouting out the words "Under God" with unblemished pride

~continued~

It was then that an elderly couple
Came to stand squarely by my side
They began to sing a song written in 1913
In my heart Katherine Lee Bates' lyrics will always reside

With our arms holding each other firmly in place
Singing so loud they heard us in the valleys of solitude below
Words written to put a shape to something forgotten or invisible
America the Beautiful we shouted from this heavenly plateau

The onset of summer sent me to this personal reflection
It does so every year when we hit the month of June
Reminiscing about that place so far away from nowhere
Pledging and singing, not caring if our voices were in tune

Speaking to me as if he were the sound of America
The elderly gentleman stated, "Young man, let me give you some advice"
"When you stand up here God hears all prayers without words
It is in this very spot I learned my faith and to compromise"

"Preach to everyone you meet she truly is beautiful
These words come from an eternal sinner forgiven twice
Politics are never means to any proper ends
But fighting for freedom is always worth the price"

"Up here you will never hear poisoned words
Do not let the beauty of this country go to waste
Like myself place yourself in symbolic immortality
Share this song of freedom with all enemies you face"

~continued~

The old man left me with a few more words
Before the three of us sang the song once again
He stated, "Life, my son, is all about the ride
Also end each blessed day with a hearty amen"

Upon this day my inner light turned on
Thanks to a gentleman who never gave me his name
I will always remember him as the voice of America
Who cherished hard fought freedoms within God's domain

Flow

Underneath the ice of time…

Within the heart of every man…
Yesterday bombarded me
With every pain that she could hatch
Pushing the bitter wind to erase my being
Your hands of love my only safety catch
            …a natural progression occurs

The forbidden reality…
Quarantined within twenty-four hours
Where an aroma of obscurity burns the flesh
Lost within the crowd of a single day's life
Yet with your smile you mire doubt enmesh
            …beauty resides within the beast

Chemical euphoria flows…
No longer indulging in the frenzy
Remembering to always forget to forget
Your touch removes the reddened paradox
Truth cannot hide to you my happiness is now in debt
            …from the stoking of the flame

Enthralled in the essence…
No longer trading air for bitter angst
Transversing the tides of any single day
The unquestionable presence of you,
my ever-opening flower
I dedicate my heart to you
That is all this simple heart must say
            …When sweet loves endorphins release

                    …for you I will always be waiting

Lover's Lane

Shall This Moment…

You go…
You have torn through all my weakness
Heating the marrow of frosted lonely bones
Leading me down passionate passages
This hollow man would never have known
 …to my head

To you I bestow…
A tear dropped nearby
As we strolled along life's path
It was a bead of joy and gratitude
For ridding this soul of ire and wrath
 …all that is me

Let my love…
There is an exhilarating sensual feel
When you reach out to hold my hand
Knowing that gravity has decided
This is the place for my heart to land
 …speak for me

You define…
No need for diamonds and Gucci
Put on some blue jeans or a faded dress
Your beauty glows from within your soul
All the way to your smile and gentle caress
 …true beauty

~continued~

May I...
Take your hand gently
To warm the cold after falling rain
Walking the path known as eternity
The dust of life blowing desire into our veins
 ...walk with you forever

... never end

Two and Ten Make One

Is this what causes desire
Could it be the prelude to a passionate kiss
Do you understand the power within your hands
Tender moments we share intertwined pleasantly reminisced

Your fingers flow through the art of me
Rubbing any leftover traces of sadness away
Gently searching my lifeline to caress jagged scars
This is a simple need that puts perfect in every day

When fingers appear to be cut to fit
When palms so perfectly unite
They become solitary human shields
Letting others see the glowing auras from our delight

Either causing a heart to pound wildly
Causing tingles up and down the spine
Or easing away all the pains of the day
Your ethereal touch is simply divine

No fight, no flight
This is love's fruited terrain
You execute abductions by taking my hand
Finding sanctuary and solitude with digits interlaced
Your feathery touch leaves me forever at your command

If only for a simple sixty-second interval
This is how two and ten become a solitaire
Let us get lost in a passionate kissing of our mitts
Please, take hold of my hand
Let us sway our arms through life
Entangle fingers sharing a wondrous love affair

One

One
One day
One lucky chance
One great classic moment
One breathe to take away

One
One smile
One flirtatious glance
One moist tender kiss
One timeless embrace to last

One
One love
One pounding heart
One feeling of elation
One dream of us intact

One
One second
One minute everyday
One memory still haunts
One love that went astray

One
One hope
One unanswered prayer
One feeling of emptiness
One everlasting moment of despair

~continued~

One
One soul
One missing touch
One need for more
One missing you so much

One
One ambition
One future desire
One day it will happen
One heart gets lovingly acquired

One
One truth
One undying fact
One need for your love
One never able to turn back

One
One day
One's dream may come true

For Love of a Butterfly

A dark omen drifts nefariously through the benighted sky
An intense scarlet crescent moon scarcely glints through
The general calls out to summon his greatest storyteller
To share the heroic legend of a warrior Cyclops
Known throughout this kingdom's lore simply as Zoo

Hoping to solidify a covenant within battle weary troops
Many united only by blood lineage and fear
All sitting quietly polishing their armor and swords
Pondering if their dedication is devout and sincere

Desperately in search of the great equalizer
Seeking how to put bravery within troop's hearts and heads
The general remembered a narrative from a time long ago
History taken from this very sedgy field
Where in the morn gallons of blood shall be shed

Upon a high rock cropping the storyteller now stood
His long gray beard whipping freely from a warm wind
Appearing frail from a hard life of bitter ale and battles
Yet his voice echoed through the valley as his tale begins

"So very long ago, yet standing in this very spot
A creature named Zoo led a mere nine hundred men
We shall battle descendents of the very evil horde
The 10,000 strong Zoo and his heroes
Buried within the confines of this ancient glen

Zoo was the creation of mystics and magicians
It is considered Merlin was the head of this pact
They all met one day upon the cosmic mountain
Each bringing a vital essence for Zoo's tract

~continued~

177

Mixed together under a storm of damnation
One by one parts were thrown into the pot
Every mystic chanting an incantation
In order to keep the bubbling blood from clot

Three hairs of a wolf were dropped into the mire
Giving Zoo ferocity of the relentless variety
The heart of a leopard was sacrificed next
For a strong forceful determination
Capable of putting fear into all of society

A bat's wing and owl's talon
Now stirred into the pots mixture
Zoo should have all wisdom and knowledge
Be able to see any oncoming dark thoughts
Standing silent guard as though a gargoyle fixture

More mystics arrived adding to this sludge
That lightning would form into their creature
A crocodile's tooth to enable Zoo to sense danger
And two jackal's eyes would make keen vision a feature

For fear that Zoo would be drawn to the sun
Venturing away from his mandated post
The body of a crayfish would keep Zoo in hiding
Within the shell of solitude he will enjoy life most

Unbeknownst to all the magicians in attendance
A butterfly was caught in the lightning's flash
Giving Zoo the ability to have a heartfelt transformation
Whenever beauty and love give his destructive soul a slash

~continued~

Zoo's panel of makers stared at him in veneration
Their creature stood more than nine feet tall
With the muscled upper torso of the most giant of men
And the four strongest legs any of them could recall

A fiery mane of blonde ran down his neck
Covering his back and all lower quadrants as well
He had the two most enchanting aqua blue eyes
Of his smile the ladies told century old tales
That one glimpse would cause their passions to swell

Assigned to guard the mists of Avalon
Keep well the remains of time's greatest king
Holding this sacred ground for the pillars of eternity
Zoo stood guard proudly through every winter's storm
Not giving any ground even during the monsoons of spring"

The storyteller stopped momentarily
A quaff of ale quenched his tired dry thirst
Every man amongst the army below
Stared with intensity
Awaiting the rest of this tale to be dispersed

"All stayed the same for over four generations of men
Zoo was always guarding the great kings remains
Then on a warm spring day with the smell of clove in the air
A beautiful young woman rushed forth through the mist
Screaming at the top of her lungs Zoo's name

~continued~

Startled, Zoo stumbled, then blocked the beauties way
Demanding what non-mortal had told her of this place
She stated with pride she was from the lineage of Guinevere
Proclaiming her name to be Butterfly
She kissed Zoo and took him into her embrace

All the mist cleared from this ancient aisle
Sunshine pelted Zoo's body and face
Then as if he were sprung free from a cocoon
Zoo transformed into a normal member of the human race

Butterfly stated she was told long ago
By a wise storyteller who mentored many kings
That if she wanted true love, she had to kiss a horrid creature
For within his essence were chrysalis and imago wings

She came to visit the first of each spring
Kissing him fresh to bring his human form anew
For the spell only worked if his feet were upon this aisle
Within winds distance of the dead king's view

Upon the sixteenth spring of Butterfly's arrival
Zoo's serenade of sorrow began
She did not arrive with golden lips of magic
To transform Zoo back into a man

Remembering the glittery smile within her whisper
Her eyes were crystal balls full of life's zest
Having tasted love from the sweetest of cups
Zoo broke his accord of eternity with his makers
Finding his beloved Butterfly became his only quest

~continued~

Zoo's travels led him through many burnt out villages
Sword and spear ravaged bodies at every turn
Finally he braved to knock upon castle gates
From a bearer of pain he learned Butterfly's fate
It was not that his love had been spurned

This lone soldier informed Zoo they had been invaded
By an evil monarch and his army from far away lands
Sacrificing the beautiful Princess Butterfly in this courtyard
To force the masses to meet all of his sinister demands

Zoo let loose a curdling screech of a yell
His roar could be heard from miles away
He will punish this man, this architect of his pain
Announcing for those who would care to join him
It had become this destructive souls descension day

Zoo asked not for any sympathy
Nor did he beg for the playing of violins
He only asked for when he comes to sleep eternal
To be forgiven for all of tomorrow's sins"

The storyteller stopped again for a moment
Sensing the tensions rise from all around
Taking another sip from his quaff of fermented barley
Not a man in his presence uttered a single sound

From this very rock the storyteller screamed
Zoo called upon the nine hundred before him to fight
They were warriors, farmers and boys in their teens
With the lone mission to turn a wrong into a right

~continued~

"I am here before you neither man or beast
Yet I possess the aching of a lonely broken heart
I loved your Princess Butterfly more than any creature alive
So much in fact I allowed my life of eternity to depart

Being mixed of the bone and blood of many a creature
There is no fear here knowing it is time to bleed
Follow me closely into this battle of mass destruction
We shall crucify the evil monarch and his minions
Putting an end to the spreading of their demonic seed

I beg of you all to close your eyes tightly
Knowing that after tomorrow, tomorrow's may not come
Give yourself this night as a refuge from reality
We shall have the sleep of the just until the dawn breaks
Then the monarch and his masses shall succumb

Each of the nine hundred considered his choices
The thoughts of destinations and futures undefined
They all believed Zoo would be the last warrior standing
Being tenfold outnumbered never even crossed their minds

As the sun arose the nine hundred and Zoo
Raced across this very meadow with pride
In an amazingly brutal and effective way
Each member of the Monarch's army died

Trying to get away from the creature of death
The Monarch fell from his mount
Zoo pounced upon this devil in flesh
Torn into five hundred pieces at last account

~continued~

Each of the 900 stood still in awe
Not a single one was required to draw a sword
They all knelt down in front of a crimson covered Zoo
Their faith in humanity now being restored

Zoo's only request of those by his side
Was to remember the beauty of butterflies
To find love in each and every one of their hearts
Perform acts of mercy in plentiful supply

I now must return to my mandated post
Begging my masters to allow me to stay
In order for each of us to remember the honor of today
We shall tattoo our army's arms with that of a heart
With butterfly wings to show it the way"

The storyteller sat down upon the rock
Exhausted from reiterating such a long tale
Those in the front were amazed when he turned
His arm tattooed to a matching detail

The King announced they too were outnumbered
But Zoo and Butterfly watched over this hallowed ground
The blood relatives of those slaughtered here long ago
Will run away from the pride and passion we abound

That very next morning the army of the monarchy fled
Just hearing the battle cries of the King's angered men
Zoo heard the cries through Avalon's mists
He sat smiling, holding a ripening cocoon
Awaiting the spring with a glow in his heart
For the arrival of his beloved Butterfly once again

Heart's Keep

Winding trails of many quests...
The acrobatic movements of a fanatic heart
Adrenaline anxiously pounding through the veins
Morning's sunrise brings the end to another night with you
Dedication to this dream is what helps me sustain
> *...begin long before I arise*

Dreamy aspirations of life's focal point...
The honeyed tastes of your sweet comforts
A most sacred emotional nighttime treat
Leaving buds craving for memories of tomorrows
Feeding each other chocolates when we first meet
> *...are found during the closing of my eyes*

Until the morning sighs her first breath...
Blinded no longer by this nocturnal spinning
An unconditional slave to the habit of sleep
No longer nervous about this squeezing euphoria
It is undeniable you are my heart's keep
> *...The one I am longing for is in mind's view*

Under the influence of your power each night...
Please love every ounce of me in slow motion
Feel the glowing bliss of a hand holding you true
Beyond the horizon there will be a day that you lived
Within reach of these eyes which your caring and devotion
Always manage to alter into a lighter shade of blue
> *...Always waking to another romantic dream of you*

I Am 2

Your first trip to the mountains
You hiked 4 miles strong
Little legs carrying you step by step
As you loudly sang *The Sharing Song*

You gazed in awe at your first waterfalls
Constantly wanting to don your "wimming suit"
Happily fed chipmunks and ducks your lunch
Always wearing your adorable hiking boots

~continued~

The look in your eyes when you realized
Boulders were just gigantic rocks
Yet you still wanted to take them home
Saying they will fit in your pockets and socks

Your brothers have a big stake in you
It is obvious in how hard you play
Constantly covered with dirt and grime
As you heed every word that they say

The way you answer questions
Like when someone asked, "How are you"
You give them a great big grin
Hold up three tiny fingers
Proudly announcing that you are "Two"

A trip always to be remembered
The mountains were a reverence for you
Holding daddy's hand, walking along
Staring intently at Mother Nature's offerings
While glistening with your eyes of blue

As an old man I shall always remember
Endless happiness flutters about my head
The simple things you have done and said
You are this soul's daily bread

We Call Her Mother

Of places for streams of meditation
A wayfaring stranger strolls by and speaks
His soft, breathless melodies
Tell of his mother's gardens, plush and deep

He says there is a magical iridescence
Just watching the falling of autumn's leaves
Aerial boundaries of rainbow spectrums
Upon the simple task of cleaning out ones eaves

He claims the allure of sanctuary
Lying silently still upon a paradise reef
Staring intently into horizons beyond
Caressing thoughts of stress relief

She has been here since inception
She is pure power and energy
She is in your mother's garden
She is the tide that moves the sea

He orates of mystic places
With buoyant spirits, tranquility
Claiming the aroma of sweet scented streams
Is the dessert of life, his mother's nativity

A different kind of freedom,
Proudly he proclaims
Is the abstract care and pattern
Of watching the moths dance
After a cooling September rain

~continued~

A thirst is quenched when she speaks
She is a harmonic whisper upon the wind
She is the mist of the perfect waterfall
All that grows her sword defends

This stranger utters his mother is the liberator
Causing a shift of consciousness to all
His mother's name is Nature
A serenity of life
Winter, Spring, Summer, and Fall

Dew Drops

If all things that glittered...
Dew covered blooms sparkle in the morning sun
Their every move radiant in a soft blowing breeze
Each drop representing a sweet memory we share
Reminding me eternally forward I move towards you
Crawling proudly upon scarred and wounded knees
> *...were captured within our dreams*

Would we find joy in the emptiness...
Life does not always turn book's pages to Neverland
Depend on me to help get you through your darkest days
Use my body to warm all your heart's aches and chills
No medication required if with me you would slowly sway
> *...of hearing the wind's screams*

When the deep sighs of moonlight...
As you sit alone staring at a cloudless night sky
Be cognizant your beauty is in the forefront of my mind
From far away I see the same magical falling star you view
Its exquisite shine reminds me of a place I hold dear
Sitting next to you, whispering a ballad with our fingers intertwined
> *...flow as a ballad for your tumbling tears*

Know that my heart is still held by you...
For all of the beautiful things you are each and every day
Acknowledging with you is the only time I truly can be me
A new soul will be born the day the two of us become one
With just one pleasing taste of your lip moistening dew
My precious bloom let us stroll off together in the morning sun
> *...as my arms long to hold you near*

Ember to Flame

So little sustenance available
Hovering just beneath heart's plague
My marrow a sun-faded color
Unfinished sympathy pensively vague

Living within a valley of solitude
Inertia creeps as the birds bustle away
Drowning within an endless vortex of sorrows
Agony destined to be every act of this life's play

Suffering through too many sandpaper kisses
Visions blurring heavily in black and white
In you rode upon a glistening melody of rain
Causing my soul's embers to ignite

Much time has passed since my first glimpse
At the sugar cane fields within your being
Suturing pains chasm's with golden thread
The spirit of my seed no longer fleeing

The clock has ticked ninety million times
Since your friendship became my dove
My walls of silence heeded your souls singing
Time has become the evidence of our love

Now is time to feel the rush
Pleasures should now be sown
From this passion we have patiently reaped
Urges a mere humbling of my deepening love
Calling for your kisses long and deep

~continued~

Baptize me in your decadence
Give me your lust in a steady supply
Please dance with me your erotic dance
Within the darkness between fireflies

Walls of silence shattered with your arrival
My words now forming from thoughts of your flesh
Hands aching to be placed upon your hourglass
These lips of fire feverishly longing to mesh

Swallow me with your torrid desire
Demand from me my essence and soul
Cuddle with me in a sweat drenched heap
My flames for you are now burning out of control

Inhaling Life

Just underneath the dust free windowpane
Lustrous silver moonbeams
Perform a rhythmic butterfly dance
Upon the top of the solid oak antique desk
The smell of fresh lemon-seed oil aimlessly adrift
Combines to leave me momentarily in a trance

Bound in the softest black Corinthian leather
On the cover a single Carmine rose is embossed
This journal sits perfectly just left of center
Right next to rosary beads and an old golden cross

Sitting now at this pristine healing place
Running nimble fingers gently over the cover
This diary of dreams and pains still holds unconscious powers
Reading once important thoughts long ago forgotten
Leads to a replenishment they are newly discovered

Once the ink in the well led to unending strokes
Detailing each significant moment of bloom
The papyrus could sing every echo of the heart
Halfway through this journal turns dark
Her departure transformed elation into gloom

This journey ends a heart plea story
Yet started with violets in hand
Traveling from midnight dreams
Through the frustrations of being a human piñata
Slipping and descending into harsh demands

~continued~

Closing the book with a feather touch
Eyes saturated from reading past scars
Thinking it is time to sterilize this wound
Search for material sanctuary staring at stars

Closure is not about finality
It is time for a new beginning to spark
From within the desk drawer a fresh journal is lifted
With inkwell refilled now is the time
For the rest of life's cruise to embark

Overtaken with wild visions and thoughts
Suddenly feeling freed to dance upon the ledge
Knowing now why all poets do not dream of angels
Romantic interludes can lead to a soulless dementia
Driving through one's heart with a hammer and wedge

Time for an exodus of relationships past
Yesterday's shadows transform into remnants and fade
I can finish that ballad that never was written
To a periwinkle sky I shall serenade

This illogical spiritual transformation
Shall not lead to debauchery or vice
Choosing to no longer lounge upon the mantle of suffering
This rush of deliverance strikingly profound
Just inhaling life for while will suffice

The Power of Mango

Across the frozen candle
Held still by the breeze that did not blow
Your silhouette the embodiment of sweet divinity
Skin glistening of stardust and fresh fallen snow

Your hair is filled with peony and lotus
Emitting your ambient purity and beauty renewed
Within your extended hand, a single buttercup blossoms
A promise of your body's riches, soon to be grasped
Telling me liquids of passion will be spewed

Gliding into light and knowledge
My thoughts pursy as is my breath
Not sensing this nights bitter chill
Anticipating our passion eclipse

There is no dance of doubt or fear
My skin set ablaze from your telescope eyes
Heartbeat paralyzed by your salacious appearance
My rapture of lust to be your claimed prize

You motion me close
Touching my arm
Galvanic bumps arise upon my skin
Into my ear a whisper from you
Sibilant as to your desires
Kiss me you ask, you are contagious
Feverous with sexual fires

~continued~

Grabbing a fruit from the table
A mango juicy and ripe
You take one bite
Sweet sugar flows down your chin
Your grin of sexual delight

Crazed by your flesh
I crawl into you
Surrender your only command
Your primitive nature liberates my beast
As sweat pours and throbbing expands

Feeling the power of your dark divine
Luxuria consumes both our bodies and minds
Begging me to stroke your velvet
Until our bodily fluids become intertwined

Rapture
Explosion
Gravity takes control
Bodies limp from our physical spree
Nefarious thoughts
Knowing seconds soon will occur
As we sip on a nice dry Chablis

The Willow Will Weep

Shapeless hesitation
A moment of deja view
Devotion grabbing memories
Pints of poison bubbling renewed

Looking back in time
Envisioning hues on white
Unable to see what your canvas hid
Truest colors never fully within sight

Swerving to avoid your vapor
A letting of darkening steam
Half of my mistakes, actually maybe all
Were reprisals to verbal attacks
Made upon the self-esteem

Walking down this street
Seeing a face so similar to yours
Reminded me to tread carefully
When approaching a cesspool of hate
Always step with a wayward curve

I held unfaltering
To my sword and my cross
Hoping valor and honor would sway
The branches of your tree
To follow my hearts wend
Bending your feelings my way

~continued~

Somewhere in my past
Silly thoughts did abound
Constantly hurrying up slowly
To pollinate your fertile ground
Sharpened perspectives realize now
The sun does continue to shine
The tide does turn when the moon wakes
Even the wind continuously sings resplendent songs
Without your sharpened wrangling around

Leaving me lonely and colder
Your verbal rain showers full of grotty debris
Remember your verbal onslaught
Claiming with a sniggered laugh
Not even a willow would weep for me

Running to a standstill
Precious details giving way
On this boulevard of broken dreams
Fear in the belly receding
It was not your face I have seen this very day

Commando

Strolling along
Feeling extra smooth
Headset blaring
A funky 70's groove
Free to decide
Pure genius abounds
Life is a beautiful cage
Second chances all around

Today I love everybody
There can be no regrets
Earth Wind and Fire blaring in my ear
Setting free my mental debt

Filled with this spirit
Soaking in the sunshine spray
Tearing through my own weakness
No cloud-cover bringing gray
This moment is mine
September swings my way
What a breath of fresh air
I wore no underwear today

Connected Souls

My theory of everything
Fluttering about like a hummingbird
Placed upon your angel wings
Your sweet voice keeps apace
To my souls marrow you do sing

Holding this sentimental institution
Above what many call true love
More like a constant vernal equinox
With Iris blooms falling from above

Your smile is my comforter
A seraphic blanketing it emits
Mellisonant each syllable whispered
Immersed in every sound you transmit

Your skin soft and smooth
Cherubic, delicate in my hands
A blossoming smell of elegant simplicity
Causes my heart to throb and expand

Your eyes cause mine to spiral down
Knowing into them this man could stare
From this very moment we share right now
Until the world utters its final prayer

There will never be any downside
To this overwhelming affectionate bliss
Lovers forever, above this earth or buried below
Connected souls can never decay

The Color of Sound

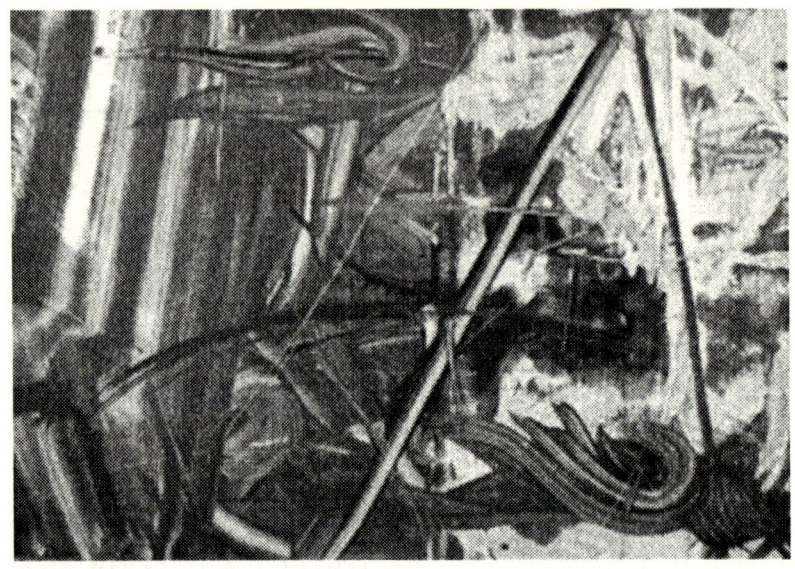

No burdens on the periphery
Where most of us can drown
Feel every beat
The chorus of souls
Let the rhythm pound

Meditations meld to incantations
Compulsion carries one away
Molding itself into a midnight groove
The vibe causing the body to sway

Hanging on to every thump
Percussion throbbing through the veins
The body a valley of whirling winds
As the music invades your brain

~continued~

Mind and body become a covenant
Stressors slowly become unwound
Making amends with the troubles of today
Inhaling the healing colors of sound

Tingles N Tears

Falling deeper and deeper...
Once thinking lovers an endangered species
I stepped into the twilight of your fairy tale
Suppressing my natural alarm from ringing
I spill to you my story in every last detail
   ...into the confessional of your eyes

Your loving gaze sedates me...
Shuddering anxiously at the thought
Promises of you ready and waiting in white lace
Revealed in your eyes amorous reflection
I am somehow your sunshine, your sweets to taste
   ...with the tingles of butterflies

Silent stares turn mellifluous...
Entranced with your slow, delicate motions
As arms hold tight, pressing cheek to cheek
Burning from our souls a moving melody
As you sing softly, words of love new and unique
   ...as your passionate whispers turn to dreams

You have taken away the lonely pain...
Moving in unison with the seasons
Now seeing time as tickling away
Endless thoughts of you within my arms
This is the part where the crying starts
Knowing that dreams come true each day
   ...causing euphoric tears to flow in streams

Angel's Voyeur

Becoming an angel's voyeur
Longing for a soul embrace
She is my last temptation
An ethereal goddess of exquisite grace

She has me under the influence
Knowing now I shall never again have thirst
Enveloped with exploding rapture
It is she who shall be my hearts nurse

Now having a second heartbeat
The rhythm whispers secrets to me
Give unto her your flesh, bone, and breath
Sparking amore's implosion for eternity

I dedicate this man's heart to you
Consider the lovelight sparking in my eyes
Initiated by the flame you ignite within my soul
My smiles for you come in endless supply

Be careful where you kiss me
Fragile surfaces everywhere
Stemming from an ordinary life
Full of lost hope, cursed dreams, and despair

I am an angel's voyeur
Her existence allows me to seize a vivid sky
Ride the waves of an endless blue sea of felicity
Ponder inner reflections that cause exhilarated cries

~continued~

Take one chance, just look at me
Nothing but sunshine bursts await
Hand in heart we can ride the colors of a rainbow
Make exploding desires our bonded estate

Welcome me to a world unknown
An intoxicating, sexy kind of passion
Hearts dancing in unison to your angelic melody
Where trust and love are never in ration

I am an angel's voyeur
Yet she has known all along where I stand
Just beyond the horizon from her window
Waiting for the day she proclaims me her man

Sunset Dreams

Shadows from palms
Criss-cross the sand
We are walking barefoot
Hand in hand

Sun is setting
Waves pound the beach
We stop and stare
There is no need for speech

This dream is a moment
A second stolen in time
Where we take in the beauty
And your eyes stare into mine

Unfortunately
It was too soon I awoke
Before the kiss could begin
And your soft skin I could stroke

The setting was marvelous
The dream had potential
For a love-affair to begin
Tonight I sleep for the sequel

The Neck

One simple sweet pressing
A nibble
The taste
Pressing the lips
On the sweetest of space
Lifting her hair
Brushing it aside
The spot on the neck
That runs chills through her side
Aroma
So sweet
Her flesh
Shampoo
Perfume
The flesh from her neck
One just wants to consume
Triggering excitement
Wanton desires
One kiss of her neck
Will ignite all human fires
A gentle pressing
Consumption
Let me feast from your neck
Heated moments do follow
From one simple peck
The spot is right there
Hidden from view
Long flowing hair
Just needing to move
Her arms hug her body
As you kiss from behind
Find that sweet spot
She will lose her control
As well as her mind

Novocain

It is not I
Fighting these devils and dust
Losing my grip
Seething because of life's lusts
Conspiracies collide
Emotions in motion
Do not answer the door
You will find my commotion
Losing my grip
Instrumental illnesses arise
I step out into the cold
Wearing a brilliant disguise
My city of ruins
This crowded head
Sick for your cure
Heart and mind in your stead
Never shall I break
The other side shows no care
Burning for you
My soul driver
I must stop to stare
Sometimes salvation
Comes in one drop
Not testosterone or alcohol
Can make the mind stop
Agony and fury
You are missing my campaign
Cling to where I stand
You are my Novocain
To make this life sustain

Bastards

There she stood on her wedding day
An angel in white pure as fresh winter snow
Her smile beamed with but one burning desire
To love this man and watch their family grow

The shining path became short lived
Soon Jack Daniels severed her life into shreds
His once wooing, cooing and salutations
Evolved into cuts and scrapes from which she bled

Shadowed words were rarely forgotten
Echoing within the red reflection of his eyes
Dissection of her pride with whiskey breath
Left her with the bad taste of being dehumanized

Dejected
Rejected
Feeling her heart had been ejected
Cycles of uncertainty left her paralyzed
The only pearl of light she could clearly see
A need to keep her soul and her children alive

Some days thoughts of liberation seem unhallowed
Imaginary friends soon helped fill her personal void
Thoughts would come from somewhere south of respect
She would find reason to blame herself for him being annoyed

Awakening each morning in a garden of torture
Upon the borderline of self-destructive blues
Realizing her head was upon the same pillow
That she once dreamed of a happy life in vibrant hues

~continued~

Thinking she would be haunted by the vision
Of him lying lifeless upon the steel-plated slab
The papers said it was a crime of passion
She quoted to them it was a fight for survival
With every ounce of energy her tiny frame could grab

Somehow she had found the strength to endure
That night concluded a long list of lasts
Last vile words, last tears, last surrender
Last fist swung with her requiring a cast

Freedom acquired with no second thoughts
No worries of staying one step ahead of her past
No regrets for the desire to be loved and cherished
Names no longer carry the edge of broken glass

Remembering that words are truly not for cowards
The threat of violence is never a reason to dance
Realizing love does not require purging flesh and blood
Those that violate this sacred entity of humanity
Earn no rights for second thoughts or the fooling of a third chance

Aphrodite

Everything in transit
Evening mist spinning adrift
Chained to a picture
A smile that gives me a lift

Waters of peace move swifter
In the spirit of her smile
Swept away by simple beauty
Her current's powers, stronger than the Nile

Breathing below the surface
Still viewing her lovely face
Fresh as drifting clouds
Floating all about the place

Satin wrapped cheeks
My walking stick when I view
Lips laid bare for kissing
Sugar's delight through and through

Eyes of simple radiance
Whispering you love me
I write this letter to a young rose
Well her picture is all I can see

Let the willow weep for me
Put a little sugar in my bowl
Do not sail on down these waters
No kiss from a picture can make me whole

~continued~

My driving force fool's fancy
This picture my only nearness to you
All I can do is cry
Your picture floated away
In the peaceful water of blue

Black Roses Red

Welcome to my dreams
They are complex simplicity
With infinite possibilities
Of what you and I could be

Walk yourself right in
Needing no light to see
Has there ever been a woman
Who could bring such sweet, sweet misery

Welcome to my dreams
You are my candy rain
A simple taste of honey
An addiction greater than cocaine

When the time has come
As slumber creeps its way in
Someone has blessed the dreamer
With your touch my blood begins to thin

Welcome to my dreams
You are my memory pain
Your scent is tangerine
Your name is in the rain

My forbidden lover
Strangers we might as well be
Forever in your eyes
A dream is all I can be

~continued~

Welcome to my dreams
Could I become a part of yours
Or should I spend my time dreaming
Wondering who is behind your door

I may never find myself
Manifested in your heart
But dreams of you turn black roses red
Even if daylight keeps us apart

Thorns

Grab a Rose with too many thorns...
For the truest of loves I would sell my soul
Nonchalantly tossing my receipt with a cursory flip
Pressing my flesh against the sharp prickles of your past
Please allow my contented heart a decelerating casual drip
> *...the pain can silently sting*

Crossing the heart and hoping to try...
Referring to ancient memories and lifetimes past
Can give one a dark jaded view from above
Believing in your actions this day with ardor and fire
Will bring a bladeless stem to this bloom of love
> *...to overlook the tines of such distant things*

Cross over to me if you truly believe...
Wishing to be the morning light of your dawns
Opening your every bud into full scale bloom
Knowing some days the clouds can diffuse my power
Does not mean these days are ones of doom and gloom
> *...no consequences accompanying my grip*

For you this heart marches to a passionate beat...
The simplicity to that which I am trying to say
With a strange perfect unity you are you and I am me
Giving each other an unconditional survey of selves
Our daily motivation will change our pronouns to we
> *...a marching Battle Hymm of love with arms in full swing*

Gently together we will whistle away...
Realizing even underdogs can be victorious
Knowing there is still so very much to learn
Ease my mind with the release of our pasts
New flowers can find the future a reason to yearn
> *...Dipping our toes eternally in love's thermal spring*

Blueberry Pancakes

An invited guest to his own inquisition
Questioned illusions of yesterdays gone
If there had been more savory than sweet
Would his angel in waiting still be withdrawn

Each month of Sunday's once always began
Right here where this checkerboard blanket lies
They would lounge right next to the hand woven basket
His gluttonous creations of taste always a pleasant surprise

The shades of his realm provided by mighty oaks
Her taste buds he had stolen from the start
Always opening up special packages to share
He would dream of new dishes as they were apart

Today he sits within his own fool's garden
Inhaling a roasted garlic and olive oil crouton spread
Realizing there is no atmosphere without her around
Not even with the renaissance of her existence within his head

Remembering the day he brought the freshest of fruits
Mixing them in a pitcher with the sweetest of red wines
Viewing her delectable lips swell as the sangria sipped past
Her eyes screaming approval at this taste so divine

Fresh air alone could never steal away
The aroma of his freshly baked breads
Nor will the wind ever whisk into darkness
The smell of her perfume embedded within his head

~continued~

Bluebirds sing a cadence of emptiness
As he recalls a passionate slow French kiss
Then invading his mind more than sins of the flesh
Of a strawberry preserve croissant he will now reminisce

Without the dreamer, is there ever a dream
Aspiring to now feel the spirit of the disappeared
Mind dilated to this gray summer afternoon
On a table in the wilderness once revered

Thinking once they were bound for infinity
Yet he could not get sweet divinity off of his mind
She stated her scars were much deeper than his wounds
Gashes he constantly hid underneath sugar coated rinds

From scratch, his goodies always filled their basket
Within this secret place her smile brought all the sunshine
It became hard to co-exist when he could not stop the rain
From soaking his rich pastries as they sat down to dine

A vehement voyage into the torture chamber within
Mozzarella and ripe tomatoes whisper chaos into his mind
Thinking maybe, just maybe, things work out for the best
His delicious blueberry pancakes would have given her an enlarged behind

So he shall sit here one Sunday each month
Raising a toast to those who are now gone
In between these trips to his most secret of places
He will continue his search for that most incredible lover
Who prepares cold lobster with an herb butter that is drawn

I Endure

I endure alone within this meadow called love
Standing stately and invulnerable like the perfect tree
Yet this symbol of strength is simply a ruse
As you have taken my Romeo's heart with thee

There was a time I would bathe daily
Within the bright morning sparkle of dew
Saturated with blissful emotions for any and all to view

Then dark clouds rolled across the sky
Transforming crystalline blue into black
Though I withstood all the lightning and wind
Now I can just find comfort within hope
Time and season will bring the sunshine of your smile back

Each time I stare out upon the surrounding land
Two silhouettes upon the horizon make me flush
One is myself, having surrendered my pride
With limbs full of flowers blooming bright and lush
The second outline appears intertwined with mine
It is you standing glorious and pristine next to me
Our roots now planted like one as they combine

There is only one remedy
One pre-planned fate of nature
That can cure this demented insanity of lost amore
I must continue to believe, as if with a blessing of blindness
That you shall return once again
To taste of the sappy emotions I pour

~continued~

Within this meadow
Yes this place where I am
Find me under the influence of nature's moods
You may have left with a reason
But here I remain firmly planted
Awaiting the return of this Romeo's heart
Upon that day we have a fairytale romance to conclude

My Teardrops on Your Rose

Waves of blissful stillness
Little visions of romance
Pictures and postcards I hold
Remembering our final dance

Someone forget to mention
When it comes to matters of the heart
There is no lifetime guarantee
Sometimes destiny chooses
You lose right from the start

I seek no sweet revenge
Not begging from bended knee
I am learning how to live, knowing
You are more beautiful without me

We danced a marvelous tango
We waltzed, wrote each other beautiful prose
Just know when standing in your garden
That is my teardrop on your rose

Contradictory reflections
Your photographs and letters I still adore
With my hearts ambient extraction
I dispiritedly acknowledge
This man just cannot love here anymore

Cosmic Love

Through a starless somber galaxy
One day the mind was slowly floating away
Battling this haunting, recurring enigma
I would never smell from love's bouquet

Solemnity wrenched in solitude
Wishful incantations performed in full lip sync
Facing this fear that devours my thoughts
Poetic words of love just float in wasted ink

Losing all transmissions
During this flight into one's self
Lamentations of no hope are slowly hummed
Senses slowly coalescing
Inhaling causing the heart to numb

Just as the tides of vengeance
Spurred blood soaked memories into the soul
A flash appeared in the distance
A spiral nebula burst from a black hole

Erupting from the epicenter
Your skin and feathers glistened bright
Showering mud on the currency of cynics
Who never dreamed of angels in flight

Always one who imagined
The love of an angel simply a childish lark
Like finding gold at the end of a rainbow
Or grasping for a needle in the dark

~continued~

She smiled at me with wanton eyes
Green the most dominant hue
As I stared trying to find a place for breathing
Their color transformed to an incredible blue

My blind heart's perception amplified
Floating around in the great beyond
Falling hypnotically into your trance
Stammering as how to respond

Sensing my fears and private sorrow
You take me on a joyous journey of sound
Singing to me verbs of power
For this new language of love we have found

Nerves and heart become afire
Teeth meet tissue as I bite my lip
A glow from me in the darkened sky
Noticing my thoughts of non-belief
You cannot hide beautiful is your reply

Reaching for me
Pulling me close
Opening your wings to the cosmic winds
Holding steady my imbalance
Telling me love is about to begin

My senses will always remember
This Iliadic journey into the great unknown
An angel saved me, kissing my soul
Letting love's inkwell overflow

What If?

What if…
The sum of my achievements
Will not leave my conscious clear
Shaking for all eternity on fault lines
Failure the only action to persevere

What if…
The gates of dawn are glistening
With nothing but artificial lights
Full of decaying colors of censured truths
Leaving survival instincts in flight

What if…
The fear beyond headlight visions
Is more than an abysmal descent
Safety no longer found in the mundane and routine
All triumph of will withers away on bitter lament

What if…
Life's sounds are more beautiful uttered in Chinese
A second language I solemnly refused to master or learn
Maybe it would transform iron tears into sparkling cascades
Causing the minds internal storms to reluctantly never return

What if…
I awoke one morning in an English country garden
A magical siege of personal power taking control
Conquering the stampede of nightmare's midnight spheres
No more need for personal pampering to become whole

~continued~

What if…
I opened my eyes to the sunshine upon the rose
Making time a convenience for just this very day
Dreaming out loud as fresh oxygen pours into my veins
Proclaiming the world is mine to conquer and sleigh
Time to be evolve into a happiness hunter
Ending the role as life's paralyzed prey

Today Is Best

No time left to wasting
For yesterdays once more
Stop questioning the notion
In life you cannot explore

Bring a deeper surrender
Fight the tedious temporal lapse
When the daylight shines upon you
Searching for happiness requires no maps

What is your fertile rock
What brings about your smile
What causes a bright beckoning
What will make this day worthwhile

Many crossroads lie in front of us
A sentimental journey it should be
Not every cuisine tastes like chicken
Nor every broken heart full of debris

Today we make amends
Even if dazed, beautiful, and bruised
Emerge from slumber enlightened
From living today you are not recused

Everything appears white
Staring into the shining sun
Yesterdays are over
Their memories cannot be undone

Feel every beat of the morning
Be the blessing and the blessed
Tomorrow is so far away
Stay deliriously fixated
Today is the day that is best

Temptation

Chilling thoughts of ice cream summers
White satin tangos the constant beckon call
Hot cherry topped kisses within soft-spoken words
Harmonium's reeds floating dulcetly to enthrall

Flashing by with a wink and a shake of her tail
I named her temptation within the corner of mind's eye
Instant erotic alchemy became our flowing vibe
She told me she could stir my passion below the hollow
But if I mentioned love she would say good-bye

Loveless be the name of this goddess upon the sheets
Crimson thunder brings deliverance of luscious bliss
Once thinking of her as the wearer of the devil's shoes
Filling out acid wash jeans, giving rise to every serpent's head
Resisting the existence of all love, with a passionate razor blade kiss

She discovered long ago she was born without a soul
Finding wanton lust a way to remove death's embrace
A nefarious grin will traverse across her perfect face
Constantly teasing blithely with treasures of her anatomy's stiff grace

Tauntingly unzipping thigh high boots of Spanish leather
Her call is always heeded; there can be no turning back
Squealing ballads of love's demise and heinous destructions
Her lover's glass filled to the rim with thick liquid black

Shaking wildly beyond the point of rescue
With half-breaths and perpetual fury her ride begins
The air so thick the lungs feel they are breathing sand
Not able to come close to opening one's eyes
Until the rhythms of her hypnotic panting thins

~continued~

The moment of climax brings finality
Two become intimate strangers once again
A pocketful of memories drift away in silent speech
Fulfilling her physical temptations is this woman's soulless Zen

Summer took its gentle roll into fall
The lusting ice cream did slowly melt
There were days I thought her bites did taste like kisses
Until I awoke with puffed lips covered in welts

Realizing she had me succumbing slowly
To the devilish dance of her destiny's demise
Begrudgingly releasing the hold of this lust named temptation
Or forever fall from the throne soul filled love can supply

From Me to We

Ticking away the medicated minutes
This synthetic generation gravitates to the null
Regurgitating their guts upon styrofoam plates
Living bumper to bumper inside their skulls

Would you continue to lay your wagers down
If there were a painful death for each and every sin
Or is it with today's advanced communications
Your atonement gets text messaged by your next of kin

Are all of our current intellectual pearls
Nomads who dine in alleys wearing only one shoe
While we all continue to vacation at Miseryland
Living as replacement parts for a batch of Prozac stew

Everyone has been caught in the act
Allowing the distant future to wither cliché
Thinking the author of life's elocution lesson
Will arrive only two six-packs and a shot away

Shall we all just burn off into the distance
Closing the door upon our own tears
The embodiment of stillborn tongues
Letting a litany of words fall upon deaf ears

We cannot live this life forever
Decency rolling from the earth
Waiting for someone else's bright sunny day
We need to tell each other where it hurts

~continued~

Shall we all wake at first light
Screaming as if with one final breath
A united voice so strong it carries its own crown
Changing headlines with our last emotions
Vocalizing we are free of the me generation
Until they cut each of our skinless bodies down

Mojito

Officially pronouncing myself guilty
Thinking the definition of love was regret
Not realizing the heart itself a phoenix
Rejuvenation occurring the moment we first met

No retardant could ever extinguish
What was once thought a secondhand heart
Dancing fairies now sing soothing ballads
Hymns to the very night we got our start

Steering me upon a passion quest
Wild strawberries flowing within your hair
Candied apples are your cheekbones
Now that a smile is your constant flair

A long drink of mojito reminds one
Of the special powers of your lips
Yours tasty kisses causing senses to coalesce
Fresh sugarcane cries out you are sweetened
While rum stimulates the power of your pressing caress

May our lips never be woven or sealed
To communication or touching tongues
My vice has become the softest place on earth
Perfect lips from which everlasting love has sprung

Enchantress

A waterfall enchantress…
Where the long shadows fall
Hidden strangely within plain view
Flows a stream of living wisdom tears
Pooling into resplendent memories of you
    …balanced in liquidity

Grace without any limits…
Vibrations from your soul wings
Cause comets to write the sky with flame
Flowing letters into a one line drawing
Proclaiming heaven is your true name
    …sweet as the fruit from the clementine tree

Reawakening hope's desire…
Inner beasts no longer do battle
Past pains no longer contracted by pedigree
Now a juggernaut to your songs of lust
A deep, slow moving, soul filled potpourri
    …in the voice of my blood

A castaway to your sunlight…
There is no way I could ever truly miss you
Even in your absence I feel completely whole
Memories arouse your beauty in dreamsight
Your smile is forever etched upon my soul
    …you are the square root of me

The Needle Has Landed

Break all the silence
You will not see me down
With wisdom and courage
I throw away this frown

Floating about to anywhere
Gravity completely gone
Imagination at play
It is a brand new dawn

Please contemplate me
Come along and wish me well
The needle has just landed
I am high on life, can you tell

No more handfuls of quietness
There is a great change
No more tomorrow or yesterday
To get in the way of a grand today

I shall be louder than bombs
Sound all alarms
Out of confusion
No possible way to disarm

Constant change of color
A prism catches my dreams
On myself I will only blame unhappiness
I am standing up to scream

~continued~

This life and I
What a precious bond
Moments lost and wasted
Are moments simply gone

Unhooked from all sadness
No self-pity on which to dwell
The needle has just landed
I am high on life, can you tell

Young Love

Hello all you lovers
Let your troubles roll on by
A star shines above you
That teenage feeling shall arise

The flame
The fire
The passion that consumes
The prelude to your very first kiss
Brought about by her sweet perfume
No patience for the very first taste
Nothing is amiss
The joining must happen now
There is no time to waste

Pointless conversations
Redeeming all the same
The soul of the night engulfs you
It is the sweetest of kisses you proclaim

A moment lost
An hour passed
An evening in full bloom
All you lovers
Lose control
Lips must join for love or lust
Either would work I assume

Beautiful oblivion
Tunnel vision
Lips are bound
Twilight in the eyes of two
Upon the first sweet taste of flesh enjoyed
You lovers will not be lost
Just unable to be found

Four Words

For you I will
Four words that he states
Handing her pieces of the sky
Giving his heart to her estate

For you I would
He cries out into the air
Become a thief in the night
So you will always have beautiful jewels to wear

For you I shall
Screaming to all that will hear
Forever have a shoulder
To catch each and every tear

For you I must
Never be silent in the soul
Never blind to your grace
Always available to console

For you I stagger
Trip, stumble and fall
For one touch of your lips
On broken glass he would crawl

For you I heal
He whispers in her ear
Wash away all your scars
Forever holding you dear

For you I will
He sings out in rhyme
Forever be complete
Next to you
Until the end of time

Blue Aconite Eyes

Strapped to your heart
Holding a hollow hope
Bound by soft velvet chains
Your blue aconite eyes
Can they stare their way
Deep into flowing veins

I am the apprentice
To such halcyon days
Feeling serendipitous
Being touched by your lust
Will the feeling that life
Is finally giving me back change
End up rotting my soul in disgust

Fight for your mind
When the female takes hold
Is she belladonna in full bloom
Or is her poison
The taste of her flesh
Merely the gold of a fool

Envisioning passion's rainbow
Incandescent blue skies, after the rain
Will your kiss leave my heart racing
Spinning romantically out of control
Shall there be a bitter aftertaste of pain

~continued~

Testosterone rushes
There is no dousing this fire
Your sweet illumination takes hold
I cannot kill the flavor
Of your candy shower
Awaiting infinity to unfold

The choice is made
For love or lust
To stare the graveyard down
Opening the soul, to give it way
If your loving embrace is venomous
Please, set the jukebox on my grave

Wipe It Clean

From torn to tattered
Stone by stone, brick by brick
Crumbling pieces of euphoria
Burning hotly both ends of the wick

Another unexpected day
The water and the blood
The apostles on the street
Warn of the coming flood

All the cellophane people
Bribe the karma police
Whistling in the dark
Breaking life's sacred lease

The miseries of the wicked
Erased faces, innocence lost
Showering evil upon the pure
Not caring about the cost

Making love to the countertop prophet
Handing him stolen cash for vice
Watching him bleed, you could not wait
Not enough cash for the ice

No one can see your color
The marionette with broken strings
You are just a repeat offender
Parading as an idea machine

There shall be accountability
Unless your windshield, you wipe it clean
Or we shall see you within the bone yard
Pushing up daisies your final scene

County Fair

I finally stopped to see you
Growing pounds of self-esteem
Such a vision of beauty
That could give wings to dreams

A spell was cast
With one single kiss
The earth chanted below me
Now I always reminisce

Lips of absolution
Cherry red in look and taste
Performing weightless osculation
Timing perfectly placed

A born passenger for the emblems
Your lipstick leaves behind
Let me have it, soothe me
Your lips to mine, entwined

Falling joys my confession
Gratitude causing ego to dissolve
One kiss a ticket to the world
A lifetime of problems it resolves

You call out final kiss
This nuance not setting in
My pocket devoid of change
Your kissing booth closes promptly at ten

She Gathers My Rain

The tourniquet twists
Tear letting begins
Tighter, tighter
Covered in pain
With every wish a mirage
She gather's my rain

Out of my depth
Out of my mind
Out of my hands
I must be insane
To think there was more
She gather's my rain

When evening falls
The twisting remains
The valley of lost souls
Enters my open veins
Closing my heart and eyes
She gather's my rain

Time marches on
Tears fall in vain
Surely, I love you
Yet, You are my bain
Memories are scattered
She gather's my rain

Ambiance

Although it may sound agelessly cliché...
Fresh cut sunflowers in a night stand vase
Dark chocolate truffles for chemical release
Ravel's Bolero begins its rhythmic pound
Sensing your heartbeat begin to increase
As your mind drifts away to the sound
          ...ambiance escalates the night's advance

A rolling sea of emotions the focal point...
The scent of jasmine floats around the room
From the amethyst candle of our only light
Like a fading star it constantly flickers and burns
Dancing to the open window's breezy flight
          ...now is the time to sow the seeds of romance

Sanguine symmetry thirsts for simple needs...
Passion is everything within the written word
You view the pen and paper with sheer delight
Destination Forever the new poem is entitled
This testimony of love to you I gleefully recite
          ...feel the burn, allow the moment to enhance

Rolling slow for the full aphrodisiacal effect...
Hold me close, allow this moment to decide
Where hands will drift for their feeding this night
I have volunteered to bring you loving stimulation
Knowing painting your senses will cause the fires to ignite
          ...the ultimate collaboration of passions slow dance

Currents

Tenderness...
Sunlit shadows in white reflection
Stroking your palm with working man's hands
In the glass we are visions of window shoppers
Your tender touch leaves me supinely at your command
        ...brings ascension

Ascension...
Such sweet instigation
The first stuttering to a kiss
Lip to lip
Mouth to mouth
Breath to breath
Involuntary movement towards one another
Wondering if solid ground truly exists
        ...instills spirit

Spirit...
My eyes were closed
My mind roamed free
My heart pounded wildly with beats skipped
Under the influence of plump cherry sweets
Who could forget the first moment
We tasted the magical energy of each other's lips
        ...gives birth to emotion

Emotion...
Nothing else gives greater pleasure
Takes the spirit on a journey so just and bona fide
That exact moment when it is announced you love somebody
When electrical lips and vigorous souls passionately collide
        ...tenderly ascends the spirit into love

Sea of Love

Sun sinking low within a lazuline sky
Rejection's cold always brings forth the moon
Like blackening memories in a hurricane's eye
Hoping my mistress hears the distress signal soon

Secchi disk lowered to the abyssal plain
Stirring the benthos in hopes of drawing you near
Take me as your sweet castaway my lady of blue
You make all semblances of confusion come crystal clear

Blow wind blow
Allow the longshore current to persuade
This lady of the sea's waves to enter my pores
Crashing freely through my essence with her invisible touch
A kiss of mercy given away from heartbreak's shore

Tripton adding to her organic electricity
The tiniest of fragments cleanse the blackening away
She arrives humming canorous ballads of faith
Pieces mend as woe and heartache float away

Always answering invitations to my confessional
When I become anoxic from the desire of love's pride
Caressing me with a gentle deep azure breath of cool
Permitting her spirit spectrum to be my personal guide

Inundating my senses with her water dance
A perfect fit as her touch removes all fear
Happily drowning within my mistresses sea of love
Within her luminescence I learn to persevere

Trying to refuse consciousness as she ebbs away
Her reflection sings for me upon breaking crests
Whispering I may always return to borrow her love
Or never return if with mortal love I become blessed

Who Needs a Leprechaun

Your legends change from culture to culture
One of nature's most beautiful signs the eyes can view
No two people can ever absorb you the same
Each viewing different shades of your marvelous hues

Many believe you form a magical bridge
Connecting the earth with the heavens above
While others think you provide a mysterious link
For the living to unite with their departed beloved

There are those who take your strongest colors as clues
A prominent green can mean abundance abounds
Strong reds may mean war is upon the horizon
Where yellow shows a death for someone around

For me you bring the symbol of hope renewed
Placing warmth within the heart on a rainy summer day
With the sun at my back and the droplets before me
My eyes are blessed to view your colorful bouquet

For days that storms come from life not the sky
When nerves stand rigid and hang by a thread
Those days where there is no rain to wash away the pain
Waiting for the next downfall with anxiety and dread

Knowing your colors can stand bright
On the most forlorn and grief stricken days
Through a cracked windshield you may pop into view
Removing my thoughts to hope from life's burning fray

~continued~

Holding consolation within your shine
Placing your memory in the recesses of my mind
Just like placing you within the front pocket of my jeans
To pull out your beauty and hope at the most necessary times

Science may say that the rains must pour
For you to announce your colorful display
But I keep you with me to view at any time
Not saving you just for nature's rainy days

In an Instant

Once upon any given moment...
Constantly fighting against the hours
Feeling symbiotic against life's dust cloud
Out of nowhere you smell a bouquet of roses
Spotting a smile amongst the particle filled crowd
      ...during this fickle drifting of events we call life

The dark moments give way to a fractal light...
Scintillation beams from each of their eyes
As your breathing pattern becomes scattered
Their smitten grin cries out you will always be safe here
Testifying you will soon become all that matters
      ...leaving you marching mirthfully to a drum beat and fife

Upon that instant the heartbeat becomes allegro...
Previously crying for help to get you through each night
Forever blackening to the darkest pitch of hues
Now you claim each day it is far too early for the sky
Wile holding within your arms someone who loves you
      ...from the simple act of holding another's hand

Some, they may just "Call it Love"...
Tears of loneliness no longer run like honey
As the once invisible emotion takes true form
You besiege the masses now with a magical aura
Love can make even the coldest of days feel warm
      ...I say the heart found the final piece of its band

Euphoria

Souls relying upon autonomy...
All letters of past thoughts burning
Barely surviving the flight and the crash
Thinking the language of love a virus
Then your amative sanctum swallowed me
Refining me with your caring ways and sexy panache
...leave nights an acappella lullacry

Through your subtle manipulations...
The scent of euphoria enters with you
It is not just your Calvin Klein perfume
Your aura is beyond intoxicating
A sensual feel introduces you into a room
...I have found thrills in monolithic supply

Shriveled hearts re-saturate slowly...
Inhaling the resplendent essence of your positivity
Dancing to the elation of your trusty chords
All I hear are a melody of your scented whispers
Sanity to a once lonely chaos now restored
...mine now beats out of control

I will make my eternal paradise...
Alchemy must have bound us eternally together
Now my shadows bounce mightily with thrills
Waiting so long for the map to this treasure
Getting lost in a constant elated state of revelry
Long forgotten dreams your passions now fulfill
...within the corridors of your soul

Crazy

Moments of lessening mercies near the threshold
Broken words overtaken by a strange disease
Blurring lines of loss meld together timelessly
Undermined by moments of male brain freeze

Thinking there is nothing more rugged than love
Treacherous thoughts lead to words of pain
In these male moments the opposite of intellect
My soul's voice still affectionately cries out your name

If for some reason your silent steps
Become strong and lead you towards the door
Know we all utter things in fits of passion
Beneath our outraged exteriors
That our flashbacks adamantly abhor

Please take a brief moment to ponder
In delight remember me this way
My heart still does springy somersaults
When you say hello to start each day

In your thoughts retrieve the electrical dance
As my hands have brushed your tender skin
How I fed you chocolate covered kisses
Wiping away the excess from your chin

If in need of positive reinforcement
Gaze timelessly into the night's sky
I will draw down the stars closer to you
So their reflection can find solace
Within the sparkle of your loving eyes

~continued~

Pressure points bring about uncharacteristic speech
Being male, sometimes of words I have no clue
Hoping that deep within you still get me
Seek the truth within my eyes, I am crazy over you

Belugaloo

Sometime during my soul's long travels
I genuinely believe its path crossed a unicorn
There is no other explanation for all the healing
To my smile and heart since the day your were born

Often times
I find myself
Consumed with pecuniary items
Their frustrations make us all groan
Then with a sparkle in your eye
Fascination within your heart
You explain to me the keepsake value
Of something as simple as a collection of pinecones

It is not possible for each of us to be angels
My very own chances at wings long past its prime
Yet somewhere within my history
I must have enacted some moments of good
To bless this daddy with a love so sublime

It has been so long ago since your brothers were three
Forgotten was all the energy a small child could confine
Absorbing every breath of oxygen as if attending a jubilee
Asking relentless questions to satisfy your enquiring mind

Each morning now begins with you shouting in glee
Exhilaration abounds as you awake with your diaper dry
Then you scream through the house trying to find a taker
To sit and talk with you as you give the "big girl" potty a try

~continued~

Telling me each day with an ornery grin
You are upset daddy's cannot marry their little girls
Informing me it is my job to "walk you down the hill"
Then naming a few of each of your brother's friends
With whom you might just "give it a whirl"

Each day you inform me of your calendar skills
"Socktober Twentieff" is the day of your birth
That I should have your presents and pink cake ready
Stating tomorrow is the day of your celebration party
And you have invited almost everyone on planet earth

Your favorite animal now is a "Belugaloo" whale
Clutching him dearly at each and every night's end
But before your head hits his softness as a pillow
With nothing but the utmost sincerity
Hugging each of your brothers goodnight
Smiling radiantly as you tell each separately
They are your "bestest" friends

These days of three always come to a perfect end
To your daddy you announce grand love within his arms
I solemnly promise back to always be your mirror
Telling you of your angelic grace and beauty
Yes, daddy is spellbound by all of your charms

15 Minutes of Fame (The Jester)

It was the time of the chariot
Always the emptiest of days
Alone in the presence of my inner jester
Plato's words still causing me haze

Voice reaching the upper echelon
As the curtain slowly arose
I sat alone on the stage,
On the edge of my seat
A vagabond… in worn out clothes

The light of eternity shining
The spotlight on my one-man show
It was to be a mystery of mercy
The ramblings of a beggar
With words of wisdom to bestow

I spoke brilliantly of my journal entries
Of alibis, history, and endless lies
The audience seemed to be captured
No tomatoes were flying by

My finest hour awaiting me
Imperfections hidden under the skin
Seeing a reflection of something
My one-sided divine romance about to begin

~continued~

Alive in the moment
With outstretched hands
I felt fireproof staring into her eyes
She was sitting idly in front of me
Looking like Athena, but in disguise

The moment I lost my abandon
I saw where joy and sorrow do meet
She was sitting with royalty casually
In the comfort of a front row seat

Captured by my momentum
Taking delights in the beauty I see
I fumbled through my next statements
Causing my crowd to abandon me

This art of mob transformation
A paralyzing phenomenon of which I speak
My crowd went from combustible worship
To wanting to harm my manly physique

Stripped away of all my discipline
By a goddess donning a golden robe
My tension obviously the passing note
My own thoughts I was unable to probe

The crowd's relentless intolerance
Drew round upon round of boos
She was a conspiracy to my masterpiece
Placed within my crowd to confuse

~continued~

Her hair was golden, as summer wheat
The eyes, cut diamonds in place
Her body curved like the hourglass
Michelangelo carved monuments to her face

Knowing my time as a poet
Would abruptly come to an end
I paced slowly, staring at the sea of faces
She was now mine, I would pretend

I felt the joy, the inner peace
A few moments with crowd eating from my hand
Then sorrow came as I asked her name
"Take him away", was her royal command

Escorted to the jester's gallows
I found myself newly complete
No more acting for me, the critics all concurred
I smiled though, all to myself, knowing
The love of my life could have Ben Hur

Sleeping Angels

A habit formed so many nights ago
Special moments for this love of mine
Brief glimpses evolved into valuable hours
A doting father easily loses track of time

Show me your face as you slumber deeply
Dream until tomorrow of great travels and friends
No pictures of you can replace these moments
As I soak in your appearance with my mind's eye lens

I believe it is true
The soul of a happy child
Emits a glowing aura as they sleep
So on these adoring memory-shaking nights
It brings great joy and pride
When I sense vibrant colors bold and deep

Whispering softly, from one child to the next
Of the joy each brings to my world every day
With all that I have
With all that I can give
Know this father's love can never stray

Pictures of you
Snapshots of single moments in time
Do not show the quick changes that occur
So all these nights spent staring at bedside
Are held tight in the memory banks
Just in case the next photo taken is a blur

We teach them they truly can have it all
That they should always reach for the stars above
Yet the reason we stare at them as they sleep
Is simply because they give us the greatest of gifts
They will never allow us to leave this world unloved

May

May you find the comfort of security...
One cannot explain these galvanic sensations
An unwritten mystery that shall meet no end
When I pull you close, tightly within my arms
Our interpersonal chemistry consummately blends
      ...within the passionate burn of my embrace

May your dreams of me at night...
Wishing for nothing but rainbows and smiles
Within all your slumberous thoughts
Prior to the morning sunshine's parade
Might you feel safe within the comfort of sleep
Allowing my love to cause bad memories to forever fade
      ...cause past nightmares to soon erase

May you feel the sentimental symmetry...
The gentle interlocking of our fingers
Causes this world's harsh realities to dissolve
This bonding brings about beaming compulsions
Majestically strolling with you for the world to see
My smile becomes radiant, I am standing evergreen tall
      ...as I proudly hold your hand within mine

May you never forget you forever move me...
Taking me under with the spell of your eyes
Their radiance propels my will to give of my being
With halcyon grace your smile leaves me breathless
To an eternity within your love, I am gratefully agreeing
      ...with powers hypnotic, cherubic, and divine

Midnight Realization

Someone please speak to me
I cannot seem to find the phone
She has summoned a nocturnal creation
A beast of madness has been cloned

Ancient incantations
Rise from the bowels
Of my lovers porcine beast
The fiery tips of her fingers
Looking for fresh flesh upon which to feast

Mystery and misery
Eternal dark from day until night
Sharing her Cimmerian poison
From lips blistered with harvest mites

Breathe control in full recoil
Disintegration upon her embrace
I shriek for an angelic rectifier
To keep this heart from being erased

The awful truth of loving
Often leads to twisted debate
As I gain vision through your distortion
It is obvious you are Lucifer's soul mate

Walls inside my head pounding
Trying to find remnants of a lucid mind
Your midnight creeper growling
As the morning sun creeps through the blind

~continued~

I awake beyond obscurity
Looking at the vastness
Of the demons within your eyes
You are now the woman
Formerly known as mine
Who was a devil in disguise

Sweat

Nervous
Anxious
A slight unease
Shaking
Perspiring
From your soft subtle tease
Anticipation growing
The wait
Intense
Knowing the day will come
Leaves me tingling in suspense

In need of the passion
The movement
The pleasure
The agony of wanting
Yet waiting
Too difficult to measure
Knees shaking
Heart pumping
From dusk till dawn and beyond
The day will arrive
Our bodies will respond

Come to me
Tease me
Only as you may
Walk with me slowly
Through bodily pleasures
Please
Do not delay

~continued~

I quiver
Tremble
Shudder with delight
That you will hold me next to you
Making love throughout the night
Give me chills
Delight me
I will do the same for you
The dawn is approaching
This aching cannot be subdued

Recharge

As the inner voice crackles with static
Causing the mirrors reflection to slowly fade
Each breathing moment is so very ordinary
Life's tedium begins squeezing out sour lemonade

Time to avoid the erosion of sanity
No more waiting for the unknown
A little personal behavior modification
Shall bring rise to an inner utopian zone

The search for elusive treasures
Can start in vast field of marigolds
Lying placid staring at a cloudless blue sky
As the cadent ballad of bumble bees unfolds

~continued~

Perhaps within these desperate times
Deliverance develops sitting upon a mountaintop
Breathing in the beauty of all animate objects
The splendorous view of magic horizon's
Brings time tranquilly to an eternal stop

Could it be sanity's cure requires both feet
To be buried playfully underneath cool sand
As the goose bump inducing northerly breeze
Causes the colorful sails on the horizon to expand

Maybe, just maybe, a crystal stream
Holds the key to my heart's renewal
Fly rod in one hand, sweet tea in the other
A day spent in nature fishing
Now that might just be the fuel

Conceivably today's perfect remedy
For the return of life's infectious zest
Requires only a scant few moments
Sitting intimately alone upon a porch swing
Counting the marvelous reasons for which I am blessed

Onyx Heart

I talk to the wind
Several times each and every day
Hoping it carries my impassioned verse
To heeding ears so far away

No, she was not some waterfall enchantress
Met by chance within the beauty of nature's realm
This angel did not exhibit the proverbial hourglass figure
But she carried with her a smile that left you overwhelmed

No, she did not walk towards me straight out of the jungle
Stroking with silk skinned paws to master this beast
Yet she allowed me to dine from her plate gladly upon all fours
Desiring more and more of her delectable feasts

No, she was not some dreamed up fantasy
Yet from the Pantheon she could have easily strolled
Vibrant and confident with her every move and step
Causing me to shiver each time she stated I was the one she adored

Overflowing with seemliness, grace, and charisma
I found myself within the middle of one of Pavlov's test
Slobbering foolishly at the sight of this desirable siren
Requiring the passion her heart and soul possessed

Since she has vanished a neuron flood
Treads reality within my confused mind
My heart is threatening to commit mutiny
The thought processes all maligned

~continued~

Yes, these days I have chats with the wind
Even when the sky streams of pristine downy flakes
Uttering amorous words forged within the flames of love
Hoping they can withstand the storm
Reaching you before this lonely heart breaks

Again this night I shall converse with the wind
Wishing for my soft cadence to cross her tracks
Letting her know my heart of onyx is burning on the black
Would she please bring back her magical smile
In order for the white checkerboard pieces to grow back

Melting

Sparkling like sunshine…
Knowing where to seek ethereal refuge
Away from the raging waters that life supplies
An eternal carousel of astral romance
Aurora's garden blooms within your eyes
…poured over unspoiled ice

With you I dance…
Swaying ever slowly to a chorus of jasmine
Removing torment and tension with hidden hands
Showing me there can be beauty without any words
Shedding my soul's skin for you to command
…with tears of joy in my eyes

Removing the fears…
Every night my mind falls
Where the wild roses grow free
Encores of you on my arm my plea
Doubts that these thoughts come from a stolen soul
Yet in your garden is where my spirit shall forever be
…from elusive emotions

When it comes to love…
Ascertaining the value of holding on to the flame
The sweet taste of honey is in short supply
Cherishing the day your love broke through
The truest of lovers can never say goodbye
…I am still learning how to fly

Bittersweet Daydreams

A luminous moon upon my shoulder
The sweetest of dreams not fading
Smiling at the thought of a lady friend
She is the delicate scent of wild berries
Carried upon a susurrous gypsy wind

A carnival of voices invade my head
An anthem of discovery rings true
I once looked at life
Through an old cracked glass
Hoping to forget, then came you

The ground upon which I sit hallowed
We sat together on many a day
Watching birds fly and flowers grow
All these memories permanent cache

Once my veins flowed like ice
Until your presence I acquired
Your aura now resides inside me
Causing a flow of feverish desire

You nursed and sutured a bleeding soul
Giving clarity to a pure hearts intent
Drawing out sketches of resplendent joy
I now know not all written verse
Is hateful or filled with lament

~continued~

One would think I sit here and ponder
Within darkness, just me and nature as one
Holding, clutching a golden locket
Wishing the perfect romance had not been undone

Your star removed from the window
Leaving an ominous, dark, bittersweet void
You walked away, no visible footprints to follow
Just the memories of times enjoyed

I refuse to be a captain of dark mornings
No running away from daylight for me
You could not love and leave with out a trace
You turned this poet into a painter of verse
Showing a tattered worn soul how to feel love
And in words see beauty, wisdom and grace

Gravity's Angel

I confess of an eternal hunger
Inhaling life with visionary eyes
Walking the way the wind blows
On my way to claim you as my prize

These were not simply vague illusions
Or the caffeine hyped effect of dreams
It was under that manic summer moonlight
You kissed me deeply until my heart screamed

Having found myself wanting things
Only to watch them float right away
Then you kissed me like gravity's angel
Now my only need is for our dance to sway

What an immaculate commencement
Finding that I long for your lips as a souvenir
The heat from your soul gives me the required stamina
To march in search of you on the coldest day of the year

An unstoppable wave of walking elation
The teeth of winter's winds cannot cause me to flee
Is forever enough for me to crave one more taste
Right down to my soul, your lips put a spell on me

All vengeance shall be kept descending
My wish list quite short in its view
You flew away like time's tomorrow
Smiling, as you new my heart was renewed

~continued~

I will dance through each storm with gratitude
Keep marching forward till all daylight dies
This human machine needs one more sample
Of the galvanizing sensation your kiss supplies

One moment spent with gravity's angel
Has kept sadness five hundred tears away
Then she reach down and kissed me
Now I must search for her each and every day

Passion Speaks

Let us take it slow...
As deep as my soul may hunger
To taste the ambrosia of your satiny skin
Indulge me for just one brief moment
As I take a breath and soak your beauty in
    ...these moments so delicate and few

Allow the threat of seduction...
Every small pocket of resistance fleeting
Failure to submit now an abstract thought
Letting myself become captive to our consistency
Attached to your lips my blood rages idyllically hot
    ...to feed our lust for the taboo

Just like silver screen lovers...
Concupiscent becomes my nature
Viewing your candy store with lascivious eyes
My every move leads to your perfumed garden
Losing myself within the pleasure your bloom supplies
    ...carnal desires fuel this night's embrace

Singing out odes of ecstasy...
Kisses take the role of teardrop collectors
As the language of our passion speaks sincere
Please, do not break my fall into sparkling soul
Love, not lust, was physically spoken here
    ...within safer hands you could not be placed

Mental Emancipation

Perfect solitude
As pure as gold
No gridlock to madness
Sanity unfolds

In warm velvet darkness
Finding my way
Through spiral dimensions
Unwinding at the end of a day

The secret place
Vast and untamed
A virtual oasis
Silence must be claimed

Everyone owns this emotion
A musing of one's beast
The end of a daily journey
Eyes closed
Seeking inner peace

Locking down the shadows
Taming treason
Today's lessons learned
Erasing plans of redemption
Drift away
Harmful feelings un-churned

~continued~

Mental emergence
Return flight from the day
Taking fifteen minutes of silence
Personal conversation alone
With absolutely nothing to say

No right angles
They are meditated away
Leave these words behind me
Mental cleansing starts a brand new day

Construction of symmetry
Harmony
Eyes closed, focused on my inner dove
Taking these few moments
To recycle today's hatred into love

The More Things Change...

The final soliloquy of a warrior's soul
A conqueror's thoughts after devouring the damned
Breathing in purple from once scarlet silhouettes
Clenching tears of confusion with his battle scarred hands

Does he swim in blood as the last conquering hero
Damned to extinction by the claw of religion's facade
Swimming now amongst black boned torsos and ruins
Feeding the wolves for the unholy terror of gods

Pondering if he is even the master of his own fatalism
As he now walks in a thickening stew of revolutionary souls
Showing no mercy delivering the world from its evil
Your spirits levitation is only vainly within your control

Never joining the ranks like his brothers from history
Finding feudalistic dreams worth singing their swords
Chronicles tell our hero that Hospitallers, Teutons, and Templars
Killed infidels not only for their god, there was monetary reward

Battlefields once covered in metal carved flesh
Split open crudely by billhooks, lances, and spears
The Christians and Saracens stood strangulated faith to faith
Inevitable repercussions when deeds of hatred persevere

The shadows of selfishness have never allowed
Those that differ to break bread or drink cider and ale
One wielding the Koran, the other extending his bible
Quoting verses as the others longsword causes him to wail

~continued~

At war with the realities of a hero's lament
Knowing this epic battle of infernals will never fade
This epidemic will boil and fester until the unconscious ruins
Of the last butterfly floats off in a mushroom cloud haze

Our warrior does not give himself a victory feast
His mind's labyrinth just stumbles and stares
This world is now and has always been
Broken apart by the differing of prayers

Finding a simple purity to his sadness
The modern hero knows now what he must do
First remove his shadow of selfishness
Bid his misguided hatred a final adieu
Cry out to all that only time is the keeper
It enables one to make their inner universe pure
We all must find faith in the love of our differences
Before the future of our descendants becomes obscure

Summer

Over the horizon
On the other side of dismay
My spirit is released, set in motion
To the chirping birds I do sway

Cheese on wheat, sip of the wine
Consuming divinity seeds
Turquoise clouds
Just being alive
Sunshine my repayment for good deeds

As I find my way
To a place no one knows
Shiny things simply rivers and streams
This season in life
Brings hypnotic love
Summer is strawberries and cream

~continued~

Inhaling the grace
The essence of you
No acid turning red litmus blue
I consume your heat heartily
Use your breeze to refresh
As I hike the other side through

Mistakes and glories
Locked in the shadows
I hike alone needing no one to remind
Today I am yours
I have come for my reward
I have summer on my mind

Denial

Watching the news...

World spinning madly around sanity
Even within the lazy-boy comforts of this chair
Nightly exhibitions of the worst atrocities
Even the sweetness of solitude finds despair

Transmissions arrive via the cable
Are there truths or more lies to tell
This wrecking ball of (mis) information
Leaves a mind infected within its shell

Entering through a hall of torment
Beyond the blackest horizon of the mind
Defacing my craniums deepest umbra
Pandemonium meets the daily grind

An adrenalin rush passed through me
As a blinding metamorphosis took place
From out of the barricades of the plasma screen
Arrived the forgotten sanities of her vile face

A nefarious voice screeched out her name is Denial
Fired from the bluest lips dipped within the coldest sea
Her introduction began by pointing fingers
Claiming too many human hearts had vacancies

Each sentence she uttered calamitous
Carried from her by malodorous breath
Biting through skin like a sharp artic wind
Her words unleashing their own dance of death

~continued~

Petrified, almost comatose
Until I stared deep to see a kinder eye
Finding her oration no longer dissonant
Realizing it was sapience she desired in reply

Noticing now my calming state
No long fearing this malfunction of electronics
Her chant began with spiritual aspects
Feeling love's vibration instead of things demonic

Arrogating the deepest recesses of my mind
Denial's words removed the wedges deep within
Agitating undiscovered layers of unknown guilt
For not allowing the unified rebellion to begin

Haunting as they may be, her words rang true…

Unleash yourself as a seeker of truth
Do not idly let self-extermination onset
Never attempt to tame another human soul
Nor sit in the asphyxiation of pity or regret

Unburn all the world's bridges
Instead of finding someone to blame
Refuse to be force-fed the subversions
The talking heads in the box proclaim

Find all those who are living just to die
Whisper your poetry into their ears
Share the knowledge that becoming a dream's slave
Bares not guilt that drowns out those happy tears

~continued~

Place yourself in blind possession
Of taking on another man's cause
Bring to light with full disclosure
His suppression from unjust laws

Beyond all time
For yourself and others
Inject a lasting dose of fantasies
Hoping to turn the news at nine's tide
No longer think that it is just out of habit
You wake up and are able to survive
Begin to cross every river
Siege each second that you exist
Claim the entire world within your time
Realize your heart, words and hands can revive

Waking somehow vivified and refreshed
Bug races a soothing calm upon the screen
I remembered each word uttered by Denial
Rising to go in search of any other street disciples
Who wished to slide a monkey wrench
Into the cog's of the lie spinning machine

…or just dreaming

AND...

Like a lullaby...
As comforting as a mother's rocking chair
With Brahm's beckoning for all to Go To Sleep
The sweetest perfection is hearing you call my name
Like hearing raindrops fall euphonically within the mystique
...on a stormy night

Your voice lifts me...
Captivated by every cherubic sound
Even a giggle leaves me entranced
Wishing I could have slow emotion replay
To hear again and again your lyrical romance
...from despair

Melting my heart...
If I possessed one thousand eyes
They would all stare intently at you
Feeling the warmth of the sun on optic windows
Panes glistening from your soul of radiant hues
...like the sun on yesterday's rain

Only the sound of...
Bridging an infinite chasm of loneliness
It is now your lovely voice filling all the voids
Taken in by your sweet harmony
And the heart shaped world we shall enjoy
...an angel's harp may compare

...I LOVE HER

Slow Dance

Love is awaiting you this very moment
Enter these warming outstretched arms
Tenderly lay your head upon a strong shoulder
Sense the music's romantic rhythms and sultry charms

Do not fear our temperatures rising
Avoid that safety net of the routine
Nestle your heartbeat right up against mine
Cherish this moment as I stare deep into your eyes
Entranced so much by your beauty, with you near I pine

Rotating slowly with my lips pressed to yours
Eagerly anticipating each and every luscious taste
Allow the music to bring movement to your soul
Longing this night shall not be given to waste

Spiral downward with me to the carpeted floor
Let my hands and lips cause you shivering chills
Observe the sparkle of passion within my own eyes
Whisper to me every wish you desire completely fulfilled

Fugitive Heart

In the middle of the day in rural Oklahoma, there is no telling one small town from another. There are four buildings on the corner of Main Street and whichever state highway that runs through the town. These two-story small town high rises seem to be held up only by the empty frames of broken windows after being abandoned long ago by the promise they once held. In the city park sits a wishing well, filled with the hopes and dreams of every last resident. There is one locally owned restaurant that everyone converges upon for hot cakes and coffee in the morning, greasy onion fried burgers for lunch, and a little gossip or news of the towns high school sports teams.

Come Friday night, one corner will change. Out front, there will be pick-up trucks and Harleys, a few station wagons and a variety of other run down vehicles that survive the dirt and gravel roads that lead into town.

Spending the summer before my senior year of college working on the ranch of a long time family friend in southeastern Oklahoma, one of these corner buildings became my second home. This is where those who meet can unleash their seeds of unrest about the current market price of wheat or ponder the local political climate. We would curse about the mayor for not allowing a nude dancer club, or just drink ice-cold draft beers and count the loose bricks within the unstable walls. Yes, the local watering hole filled the boring void of many steamy, hot Oklahoma summer nights. It was at an extremely laid-back place called Booger's where nothing changed from night to night, and everyone seemed to like it that way.

One step into Booger's left you feeling time-warped into circa 1975. The brightest lights in the entire building were the Budweiser lampshades hanging above the two worn velvet billiard tables in the

~continued~

corner. One would need a flashlight to play darts within the other corner, yet several patrons spent each night flinging away, constantly knocking brick shavings all over the floor. The posters half-framed on the wall were of The Doobie Brothers, The Eagles live in concert, and an autographed picture of some Willie Nelson impersonator who played the local carnival a few years back and shared a little of his herb with those that wished to partake.

The bottle-blonde barmaid still had a smile that could charm the pants off any man in the county over the age of 30. She wore a faded blue dress that was two sizes too small back when her hair was natural. She tapped freshly polished boots to the sound of Patsy Cline as she pumped her own tip quarters into the jukebox.

The stools were solid oak, not cheap imitations, handcrafted in the local mill that was shut down after the 1980's Savings and Loan scandals in the state. The bar was home to those laid off back in the day, to bitch, moan, complain and remember the good days when their paycheck was not from their early retirement fund or good ole Uncle Sam.

In the corner, three local pastors held their own little devotional. They were discussing the barmaid's massive cleavage and imbibing their cold beer from bottles. The woman of their lustful thoughts had kindly changed the labels upon their drinks to show them consuming an alcohol free beer. These men believed she would never tell a soul of their little sinning secret; not being privy to the knowledge that she could not keep a secret nor that they were the only three in town who did not know they were the subject of many under the breath jokes.

It was my last night in Clayton, Oklahoma, the summer job fulfilled and the new college semester calling for me some 200 miles away. I would never forget the things I learned this very day. They altered the vapors of my very essence for the remainder of my life.

~continued~

He walked in with guitar case in hand, a stranger to all within the crumbling walls. His old blue jeans had rips in all places imaginable and had faded to an almost white tint from age and the heat of the summer sun. There were sharp edges to his jutting chin, loose ends to his wild rock star hair, and with eyes bluer than a clear mountain sky he looked at us all, smiled a big grin and asked if we would mind if he shared within our "100 proof love this evening."

The barmaid had her eye on him like he was fresh meat for dinner, yet she could not figure out his age. He had the body of a 20 year old, yet the scarred skin and fraying hair stated he had been around for more than just a few rodeos. The tattoo on his left shoulder resembled a velvet Elvis painting and his right forearm bore the likeness of Johnny Cash. He picked the only empty chair in the building, which happened to be the stool next to mine. He started telling tales of life and long lost loves, stories of passion and explained the four corners of our lives. This man, he called himself the Fugitive, not from the law, but from life's conformity, gave me a warm handshake and a friendly smile as he sat down.

He spoke in a raspy voice, from more cigarettes over the years than one should ever consume. The Fugitive stated that the first corner of our life force (he refused to say soul because that just made him think of singing The Commodores at a karaoke bar) was one that we totally control ourselves. This first corner is decision, "whether right or wrong, we must be strong enough to always make one." He said those that believe in the old Rush lyrics that "if you choose not to decide, you still have made a choice," knew nothing because those guys are Canadian and do not know shit about life forces. Everyone in the bar laughed heartily after that disclaimer.

His second corner was memory, claiming, "we have it, we don't always use it, we block it, we love it, we need it, but those who keep theirs selective are jaded to all things in their past and will never learn from each event within their very lives."

~continued~

283

Realizing now this dude was either full of shit himself, or just the deepest son of a bitch to walk the planet, I decided it was time to move from the light beer in a frosted mug to something a little stronger to fully absorb all he had to say.

His third corner made all the sense in the world to me. He claimed comfort as a vital thread to our very life force. "We can be comforting to strangers, comfortable with ourselves, find comfort in a clear black sky, and find comfort in love when she is blessed upon us. By choosing to stay in a place that causes us to lose our comfort, we lose our ability to decide, and to have free access to our memory banks." So now every ear in the place was tuned in, the ministers had said to hell with their ruse and started taking shots of Jack Daniels. They even pulled out their notebooks in hopes of stealing a line or three for their Sunday sermons.

The air in the room was still as all awaited the bullshitting brilliance of his fourth corner. Patiently we waited with baited breath as he consumed all the free rounds that had been purchased by the crowd.

Sensing we had all suffered enough, the stranger began his final oration. "Corner number four is quite simple, just PASS IT ON." We all looked at him with puzzled faces and lifted eyebrows; not realizing this was his plan in the first place. "PASS IT ON means, if you hear a great song, PASS IT ON, if you receive a smile from a stranger, PASS IT ON, if you are given a gift of love, PASS IT ON, never keep things valuable all to yourself. You must PASS IT ON. This does not mean materialistic things, this means gifts and giving from the life force itself, the human heart."

It was at this time, as the crowd all looked at each other thinking this man was the smartest human being on the planet and had just given us a free $500 a plate motivational lecture, that the Fugitive decided it was time to liven the joint up a tad bit. Breaking out his acoustic guitar, he

~continued~

284

busted through all the old 70's favorites called out by the bikers in the back. From Cat Stevens, Bob Dylan, Charlie Daniel's sing-alongs to a version of Landslide by Fleetwood Mac, he left us amazed at all of his talents and skills. The rough voice seemed to carry throughout the town, as if by some miraculous calling. Other locals must have felt something was going on and filed in for one drink and a little communal awe.

Realizing the night would soon come to an end, the Fugitive glowed, as he had one last special gift to share with us all. It was a song he had written long ago while he was fishing for trout in Rocky Mountain National Park. He said he hoped it would be something we would remember and take with us in our hearts. As he took one last shot of whiskey, one last long drag off a cig handed to him by the busty barmaid, he sang of his way of life and love.

Forever live those fugitive hearts
Finding not a single sunset ordinary
Letting freedom reign from no fear of fear
Sparing some love for all that pass you by
Allowing the mind to find symmetry in the contrary

The fugitive knows what a single word can do
When uttered softly with just the right smile
Orating for all those that leave honey untasted
They leave their picture frame life empty for a while

Have you ever drunk moonshine in the mountains
Taken in the countryside from the window of a train
Lived your everyday to fulfill destiny's path
From the boring nine-to-fiver do you abstain

~continued~

Do you know each and every morning when you awake
Those marvelous dreams do not have to be for rent
God bless you dreamers living out your quests
Keeping those boots from drying within life's cement

The only place to find too much of nothing
Within the sunset of a turquoise canyon sky
A true love is always beauty at every time
Not just when make-up she does apply

Knowing that all in love is never equal
The fugitive's hidden passions must always be expressed
Giving all one can, even until it hurts
Of free will and accord, not by request

Have you ever drunk moonshine in the mountains
Taken in the countryside from the window of a train
Lived your everyday to fulfill destiny's path
From the boring nine-to-fiver do you abstain

Do you know each and every morning when you awake
Those marvelous dreams do not have to be for rent
God bless you dreamers living out your quests
Keeping those boots from drying within life's cement

The fugitive sees only vanity,
Within those that hide in the shadows and dust
So one must learn to trust the voice of their angels
Passing on their words to other fugitives who feel unjust

Do you know each and every morning when you awake
Those marvelous dreams do not have to be for rent
God bless you dreamers living out your quests
Keeping those boots from drying within life's cement

~continued~

He packed up his guitar and rode off with the last hot breath of August, and it occurred to all in attendance, as we stood there speechless that he would never return. Mysteriously, a cassette recording of his speech and song from one minister's tape recorder, really hoping to steal a few lines, made it to all those that attended that night. I received mine in the mail at college some three weeks after this epiphany of an evening without a return address never knowing who blessed me with the recorded events of that night. I have had to rerecord my copy of the tape two dozen times so that I can still hear the fugitive sing upon a hot Oklahoma wind.

Photo and Art Credits

Special thanks to all of these people for sharing their talents within this body of work:

Heather Rodgers (Broken Lady 3 Photography):
http://www.pbase.com/welton/heather
www.myspace.com/brokenlady
Contributing works are on Wildflower, One Hard Winter, Morose and Blooming Muse. Also had touch-up work contributions on Nana's Voice.

Leigh Tuplin:
www.myspace.comleighleighx
Contributing work on The Color of Sound.

Flo Watkins:
www.myspace.com/flo_theartist
Contributing works on Lover's Lane and Frozen in Time.

Tonya Morin:
Contributing photo on Nana's Voice